Simple M

Trust

3

Simple Men
Trust

Hal Hartley

faber and faber
LONDON · BOSTON

CIP records for this book are available from the British Library
and the Library of Congress
ISBN 0-571-16798-5

Printed in the United States of America

Contents

Hal Hartley: Finding the Essential

There is a case to be made that Hal Hartley is the most rigorous creative force to have emerged in the American cinema in recent years. The writer and director of three feature films, an hour-long television movie, and five shorts – all shot in the same spare style, with not one extraneous word or image – Hartley is a tyrant of textural economy. For all the parsimony of his methods, however, Hartley's is a curiously lyrical, comic inquiry into the inchoate burdens of desire and duty and the elusive goals of communication and trust.

Any attempt to analyze what Hartley himself is striving to articulate seems reductive. Each new Hartley film seems part of an ongoing work-in-progress in search of philosophic resolution and the grace that comes from understanding – although as the director has averred, "Knowing is not enough." In an era in which several independent filmmakers have explored the ennui-anomie of a generation of vaguely disaffected, proselytizing youth, Hartley has been compared (by myself among others) with such contemporaries as Jim Jarmusch (*Stranger Than Paradise*), Richard Linklater (*Slacker*), and Whit Stillman (*Metropolitan*). Yet it is an earlier American director he perhaps more accurately resembles. In its meditativeness, its bitten-back romanticism, its inherent fatalism, and its casually seismic actions – a daughter's tantrum causes her father to drop dead in the kitchen, a disgruntled man in a bar laconically punches one man in the stomach and shoves another off a stool – Hartley's work raises the specter of a 1990s Buster Keaton. Where Keaton's aesthetic was technological and tempestuous, Hartley's is suburban and quotidian, but it is no less poetic or dramatic for all of that. Deadpan to the maximum, "The Great Stoneface" never smiled in his films; Hartley's characters seldom smile. Hartley shares with Keaton the knowledge that emotional precision and serene self-abnegation, not selfishness, self-pity, or

vii

sentimentality, are the correct responses to the random cruelties and injustices of the world, as well as to one's own negative impulses. Like Keaton, too, Hartley is a thoughtful—if less spectacular—manipulator of space, the prosaic geography of his films punctiliously harnessed to the concentrated minimalism of his mise-en-scène.

Born in Long Island in 1959, Hartley enrolled at the Massachusetts College of Art but in 1980 switched to the SUNY-Purchase Film School, where he studied under the late director-editor Aram Avakian (*End of the Road, 11 Harrowhouse*). He then worked with his father in the construction business as an apprentice iron worker and took a job answering phones with a company making public-service announcements in Manhattan. Hartley had completed two more shorts when his employer agreed to fund his first feature, *The Unbelievable Truth* (1989), made for $75,000. The British production company Zenith was the main financier of his two subsequent features, *Trust* (1990) and *Simple Men* (1992), made respectively for $650,000 and $2 million. The realistic yet non-naturalistic ambience of Hartley's films (he also composes music for them under the pseudonym "Ned Rifle") and his insistence on creative control suggest that he is likely to remain part of the independent sector for the foreseeable future.

Kid (1984), Hartley's graduation film, pensively depicts a young man, Ned, struggling to leave Lindenhurst (the director's hometown) in search of his girlfriend—but family ties, though tenuous, and his own uncertainty anchor him, Billy Liar–like, to the spot. Ned's sister (the "kid" of the title) and confidante bangs a stick on a railway line; a deranged man causes a neighbor of Ned's to fall in front of a car; the deranged man's sister kisses Ned and her brutish boyfriend punches him in the stomach; at the end of the day, Ned goes home with his dad. Though it was more of a sketch than a fully developed piece, *Kid* was already kitted out with the distinctive authorial touches that have evolved into a consistent style: tersely spoken dialogues and monologues (rapid-fire in the later films) elucidating their speakers' unconscious fears and yearnings with little recourse to small

viii

talk and politesse; sudden kisses, blows, and accidents; abrupt transitions between scenes; fastidiously choreographed movements and stark, off-kilter tableaux (for example, Ned and the deranged man lying on a bathroom floor by the toilet). With this first, assured small film, Hartley was already cutting to the quick.

Hartley's three features present the fraught pilgrimages of two or three central characters toward selfhood and show a couple emerging hesitantly into a relationship. In *The Unbelievable Truth*, Josh (Robert Burke), a manslaughterer who has been released from prison, hitches home to Lindenhurst and takes a job as a mechanic in a garage. Through a mutual interest in George Washington, he falls in love with the boss's daughter, Audry (Adrienne Shelly), but they are kept apart until they are able to extract the truth from a mess of misunderstandings, prejudices, and commercial transactions. Josh is struggling to come to terms with his guilt and seeks forgiveness from the woman whose sister and father he supposedly killed. Audry—her life complicated by her fear of nuclear destruction and a possessive ex-boyfriend—finds herself in hock to her father, who has tried to divert her from her wish to study literature at costly Harvard by financing her modeling career. Gently satirizing the ways in which people use money to buy and corrupt one another (the principles that Washington once stood for have been reduced to a portrait on a dollar bill), Hartley uses the Deal as his central metaphor. "You can't have faith in people, only the deals you make with them," asserts Audry. "People are only as good as the deals they make and keep." Eventually Audry and Josh make an unspoken deal to be together—though Josh's admission that he doesn't trust anyone and the whisper of "bombs" ends the movie on a purposefully ambiguous note.

That agonizing over trust led Hartley directly to his next feature, called *Trust*, in which he made palpable refinements of style, dropping the overdubbed speeches and intertitles that he'd played with in *The Unbelievable Truth* but perfecting the use of discrete, declaratory statements—and bursts of silence— to make implicit ideas explicit. (Characters speak their thoughts rather than repress or simply think them as people do in real life.) Again, Hartley was concerned with the overweening role played by parents in their children's lives. Maria (Adrienne Shelly), a pregnant and accidentally patricidal schoolgirl at war with her newly widowed mother, enters into a friendship, based on a mutual need for supportiveness rather than sexual attraction, with Matthew (Martin Donovan), a saturnine electronics technician constantly abused by his father. Tracing its heroine's progress from brat to saint, *Trust* is a melodrama – involving a sexual assault, a baby kidnapping, an abortion, a Machiavellian mom, a drinking duel, a fistfight, an unexploded hand grenade, and a lover's leap – that couldn't be less Sirkian in its droll, unflappable analysis of family violence and the moral courage it takes to defeat it and assume faith in others.

Between *Trust* and *Simple Men*, Hartley made three films for public television in 1991. Two of them were experimental shorts for the Alive from Off Center arts series. *Theory of Achievement* is a playful series of tableaux featuring a group of "young, middle-class, white, college-educated, unskilled, broke" Brooklyn adults mulling over the conflicts of intellectual fulfillment and paying the rent; it is Hartley's affectionate tribute to a group of his friends and one of his favorite films. *Ambition* is a riff about a frustrated young man's desire for professional success and the attention of beautiful women. (Its stylized fight scenes may be a blueprint for an eventual Hartley action film.) In the TV featurette *Surviving Desire*,* produced by American Playhouse, a literature professor, Jude (Martin Donovan), falls in love with and sleeps with one of his students, Sofie (Mary Ward), with little hope that she will continue the relationship. Meanwhile, a homeless woman waylays male passers-by, angrily demanding that they marry her; in romantic failure, these correlative scenes imply, lie the seeds of desperation and madness. However, Hartley gives full – if not excessive – play to romantic elation in a magical sequence in which Jude, kissed by Sofie in a bar,

---

*The script of *Surviving Desire* was published, with an introduction by Hal Hartley, in *Projections*, Issue No. 1, edited by John Boorman and Walter Donohue, Faber and Faber, 1992.

dances briefly and matter-of-factly on the street with two other guys. Needless to say, the dancers wear no Gene Kelly smiles; here is the quintessential American music number, shorn of classical artifice and genre tropes.

Hartley included a similar dance sequence in *Simple Men*, ostensibly a road movie about two brothers, armed-robber/mechanic Bill (Robert Burke) and penniless student Dennis (Bill Sage), searching Long Island for their estranged father, an ex-baseball player turned political terrorist (i.e., an amalgam of establishment hero and sixties idealist). The true subject of the film, though, is the way men look at women and seek to reconcile their various needs in them. Betrayed by his high-heeled, miniskirted girlfriend, Vera, during a computer heist, Bill tells Dennis that, "The first good-looking *blonde* woman I see. I'm gonna make her fall in love with *me* . . . And then I'm gonna fuck her"—but a meeting with bar owner Kate (Karen Sillas), a less obviously "sexy" but more earthily beautiful and mature woman than Vera, makes him question his values, specifically his misogyny and his choices of partner. As unabashedly schematic as any of Hartley's films, *Simple Men* puts its schema to brilliant ironic use when Bill arrogantly delineates the attitude—"Mysterious . . . thoughtful and deep"—that will enable him to become a callous seducer, only for Kate to praise those qualities in him when he is behaving more modestly. Hartley's films are abundant in small epiphanies like this.

Since Hal Hartley began directing, he has worked with an expanding group of remarkable actors—among them Robert Burke, Adrienne Shelly, Martin Donovan, and Karen Sillas—who have become the icons of his oeuvre, as recognizable as Michael Spiller's perspicuous cinematography. The following interview is culled from two conversations with Hartley in New York, on January 3 and March 30, 1992. On the first occasion we were joined by Donovan, one of his closest collaborators.

Graham Fuller
June 1992

xi

GRAHAM FULLER: Before you went to film school, you studied art. Can you detect any evolution between the work you were doing then and your films in terms of style and content?

HAL HARTLEY: I think so. I only did one year at art school, and at the end of that year they would have asked me, "Do you want to study painting, sculpture, or whatever?" I was very undecided. I was intrigued by fine art, but my skills were in graphic design. Anyway, I used to like to draw pictures from copies of *Sight and Sound* that I picked up in the library. The photos always seemed to be so alive and dramatic—and, in fact, they were dramatic, because they were scene stills.

FULLER: Anything in particular?

HARTLEY: Oh, I couldn't tell. I never really read the articles. It's possible I didn't realize I was looking at a film magazine at all. But I'd make drawings and paintings from them. I began making films toward the end of that year at art school. I took to it immediately. They weren't narrative films, but I had a definite inclination to focus on faces and bodies; hugely, imagistically, not story-wise. And that's something I keep coming back to, this far along. In my films, finding what really excites me about an image almost always leads me back to the human body, the human face, hands.

When we were making *Trust*, my cameraman Mike Spiller and I would ask ourselves, "In every image we make, what does the human body have to do with this picture? How does this picture gain its significance from the body in it?" Even in landscape shots, we were thinking of how to show towns—that particular Middle American kind of town—without having to get away from a human being. We might show someone walking by a bunch of power plant wires and fences and whatnot, simply to convey a sense of the landscape graphically, in juxtaposition to the human form.

FULLER: You favor tableaux, too. There's a striking interior shot in *Trust* that shows Maria talking to her mother and sister, with Matthew hovering behind her left shoulder.

You can't see all of him but you can feel the weight of his presence.

HARTLEY: Yes. The camera is pretty much entirely on Maria. Her mother is behind her. Her sister is off camera left. And Matthew is pretty much off camera right, but you can still see him.

FULLER: That elliptical treatment of the human body occurs in Robert Bresson's films. There's a compositional austerity in your work that also reminds me of Bresson.

HARTLEY: I am very affected by Bresson and, more and more, I am consciously using that knowledge – whatever that means. Sometimes it's just an emotional clarity that I sense in his films, that I try to bring to mine when I'm writing. When I'm shooting too. Bresson cuts right past everything that's superfluous and isolates an image that says exactly what it's meant to say.

In *Surviving Desire*, I show Jude's hand reaching across a table to almost touch Sofie's hand. My treatment of that action struck me as Bressonian. Recognizing that the gesture itself was expressive. Nothing else was needed. It's about getting rid of the superfluous and the presumptuous – that's what keeps coming up in my notebooks. A lot of my experience over the past four or five years as a filmmaker has been in finding out what I need and what I'm going to look at in order to tell a story. And this approach of getting rid of what's unnecessary requires being totally alive at the moment of photography. I always thought that this particular shot in *Surviving Desire* would be done in close-up or two matching singles. I thought it was their faces that were important at that moment. But it wasn't. It was their hands and nothing else.

FULLER: What do you mean when you say "presumptuous"?

HARTLEY: Assuming that there's a certain way things are done. For instance, assuming that you have to shoot a love scene in close-up. But why not play a love scene in long-shot, from two rooms away through the door?

FULLER: Is that to sustain your own interest in it, or is it because you're bored with the clichés of film grammar?

HARTLEY: They are related. I am an audience member as much as anybody. My job on the set is to represent the potential audience, a crowd of people pretty much like me. If it's boring to me, most likely it'll be boring to them.

FULLER: You seldom bother with establishing shots.

HARTLEY: Establishing shots tell me nothing except where we are. "Where we are" will be elucidated entirely by what the actors are doing and experiencing. When I look at films made even sixty years ago, it seems establishing shots were redundant then too. For instance, when I look at Carl Dreyer's films I see an extreme insistence on the idea, from one frame to the next, of the character's experience to the exclusion of all else, including establishing shots.

It's true, sometimes you *do* need a little relaxation between scenes. You can't always express an idea in a scene and then go right to another that encompasses a new bunch of ideas without a break. You need a rest. That's something I think about a lot, and I often decide to put in something a little less insistent. Five or ten seconds of something a little easier, so that the audience can digest an idea. But it has to be the right thing. Not empty of meaning.

FULLER: You also dispense with the accretion of plot information that a lot of filmmakers feel obliged to provide.

HARTLEY: Well, I think it's always there. For the most part, the feature films I've made, even up to *Simple Men*, have been based on a fairly traditional, classic narrative structure. I used to have it worked out like a map. But it's blurred now. I believe I was taught that a conventional classic American film was to have sixty-four scenes with everything in its place. Introduction, exposition, inciting incident, false climax, true climax, reversal, and denouement. It was math. A way of structuring the raw material.

Trust was built on that structure too. But once I got the story worked out on that schema, I started screwing around with it, doing damage to it, trying to achieve, moment by moment, what it was I wanted. It's emotional from this point on. If I feel something is lagging or moving too fast, I adjust it. I add scenes. Move scenes around. Whatever is needed to make the thing interesting. But I have started from a fairly traditional dramatic structure on all of my features.

FULLER: How elaborately do you prepare your movies in terms of the visuals? Do you storyboard?

HARTLEY: No, but I do diagrams. It's sort of like engineering. By the time we get to the set to shoot, all the technical crew have these diagrams of the proposed setups. It helps everyone know what to expect. And it helps me prepare for the technical implications of my ideas. This was important on *Simple Men*, where Mike [Spiller] and I knew we would shoot the entire film—with the exception of two shots—on the fifty-millimeter lens.

FULLER: What effect does that give?

HARTLEY: Consistency. Consistency of depth-of-field, primarily. Pictorially, it lends a cohesion to a movie that I like a lot. All the hundreds of images that are placed side by side to make up the movie are all seen through the same eye.

But my relationship to a particular lens is really a commitment. The scope of what the fifty-millimeter lens can see in a given situation forces me to wrestle with the physical environment I'm shooting in. If I discover I need to see more of the room, I can solve the problem by either slapping up a wider angle lens or by moving the camera back a few feet. But sometimes there's a wall in the way. So then I have to reimagine my shot or break down the wall.

FULLER: Do you see a day when you'll move the camera more?

HARTLEY: Well, I do in fact have the camera on the dolly about eighty percent of the time. There is a lot of small movement in *Trust*. But there's larger small movement in *Simple Men*. Whatever's appropriate. That's my rule of thumb. I've never felt that I've lacked the means to achieve what was needed for the story.

FULLER: Do you move the camera more in *Simple Men* because there's more *travel* in it than in your other films?

HARTLEY: I think so. The fifty-millimeter is not a wide-angle lens. Often, if I want to shoot a scene without cutting I have to design the shot to move amongst the actors.

FULLER: This kind of camera style, though, is happily unobtrusive in your films.

HARTLEY: I think that with *Simple Men* the audience might get the feeling of being "around" the characters more.

FULLER: Do you write your stories as screenplays? Is that how they get their first exposure?

HARTLEY: They start in my notebook. I write about a character, about a situation. I ask myself questions about the characters in particular situations. After a couple of months they begin to flesh themselves out.

FULLER: Do you surprise yourself with the direction they take?

HARTLEY: Never when I'm writing. But they begin to develop in fascinating ways in the rehearsal stage, which, I'm coming to realize, is just the very furthest stages of writing, where each character that I've written on the page actually takes on a life, becomes a real human person on a day-to-day basis. The actor is then putting things into it, and even at that point I'm still bringing in extreme stuff. And then, in the best circumstances, I'm always surprised. We had a very good rehearsal, actually, with Martin [Donovan], on *Simple Men*. His character, who's called Martin, was very sketchily written. But through rehearsal, the character became much more interesting. It became very clear almost immediately that there was a lot more potential there. Before the day was out, I had a totally different idea of who this guy was and what his significance was to the story. This happened without changing hardly any of the dialogue. Martin's significance to the story is that he is *in love* with this woman, Kate, who lives alone, and he is very protective of her. And when the two brothers, Bill and Dennis, come along, he's this kind of wall that they've got to get through, particularly Bill. I didn't see this so clearly when I wrote it.

FULLER: Do you normally allow the actors to develop their roles beyond the text?

HARTLEY: I don't know if I would have given myself that license with *The Unbelievable Truth*, because of the financial constraints. Sometimes the actors would ask questions or bring up ideas, and I'd say, "Oh, I'm sorry, we just don't have the time to talk about this; just do what I tell you to do." But, luckily, they did what they thought was right anyway, within the constraints I imposed.

When the whole job of making a film is not just surviving, getting the film in the can, then that line between what's writing and what's rehearsal becomes a lot less difficult to cross.

FULLER: Do you allow any room for improvisation?

HARTLEY: No, because I've never found it to be effective. I allow myself to change some lines if it seems appropriate, otherwise I'd never get it right. But full-fledged out-and-out improvisation has never, for me, yielded anything effective.

FULLER: Do you re-write at all during production?

HARTLEY: A little bit, out of necessity. Sometimes it's a word or a response that worked fine on the page or in rehearsal. But in a particular kind of daylight beside this particular tree it no longer seems to be right. So I change things. I leave myself open to that possibility more now. Largely because I can afford it.

FULLER: How do your stories come to you?

HARTLEY: I write a lot. I have certain key ideas about situations and characters and they evolve out of each other. Filmmaking for me, like writing, or having a conversation, is a process of thinking. The more I do, the more I think about. Although a lot of *Trust* existed before *The Unbelievable Truth*, there were certain ideas that I felt were half finished in *The Unbelievable Truth*, things I had discovered in the process of making the film, things that I wanted to expand upon.

I was making this film which I thought was about commerce and personal interaction, and how they are kind of corrupted by well-meaning but difficult to assess needs. The actions are those of two people, Josh and Audry, who have been separated in a *Romeo and Juliet* type way, but are finally reconciled. But there's a scene at the end where Josh picks Audry up and says, "I don't trust anyone," meaning her as well as anyone else. But then he kisses her,

and it's almost as if he should be saying, "I love you and this is a happy ending."

So do love and trust necessarily have anything to do with one another?

This is a good example of how things change. It's not how the original script was written. But by the time I got to shooting that scene on location I knew a lot more about these characters and I had this vague dissatisfaction with the scene. I think we even shot it as written, but as we'd do another take I'd change the lines and say, "No, say this instead of that." Then I finally stopped for five minutes and wrote down about eight lines of dialogue on the back of an envelope. I gave it to Robert [Burke] and Adrienne [Shelly] and they immediately said, "Yes, this is definitely it." We couldn't summarize what this meant. We couldn't paraphrase it and I still can't. It just hit a chord and made sense of everything in the movie; it provided the glue that made the rest of it stick together.

That idea of saying, "I don't trust you but I love you," is some kind of ironic dichotomy. Maybe something essential to human nature. The reconciliation of opposites. Whatever it is, it's where *Trust*—which had only existed as a plot outline with no real emotional connection for me—took off. At that point, though, I could've taken any story and attacked it from this new perspective. There was something about Josh lifting Audry up and effectively saying, "Now we've gone through this ridiculous charade, this whole movie, and I'm not going to take anything for granted ever again." That's how Matthew and Maria begin in *Trust*. Maria, particularly, is a full-blown personality at the beginning, and she gets hacked down to zero, and has to start all over again. She learns to read again. She takes nothing for granted. That's why she sleeps on the floor instead of in a bed—she's eliminating everything that gets between her and the actual experience of living and breathing, of becoming an aware human being.

FULLER: Do you feel that dichotomy between loving someone and not being able to trust them is resolved at the end of *Trust*, or do you think it's still being explored in *Simple Men*?

HARTLEY: I'm still working it out. But I worked it out as far as I possibly could in *Trust*. I think of *Trust* as Maria's movie and in it she manages to define herself and make decisions for herself and, in fact, walk right past all sorts of very real limitations. When everybody runs out of the factory because Matthew is in there threatening to detonate his hand grenade, she actually walks right into this no-man's-land, as it were. She goes where no human being should be expected to go, and comes back, having saved someone's life. She has demonstrated a selflessness so complete it obliterates dichotomies.

The balance of *Trust* is this sort of yin-yang thing. Matthew decides he wants to live only for Maria. Maria wants to live only for Matthew. Two completely different personality types complementing the best in each other. The reconciliation of opposites. It surpasses even their being together physically, because Maria comes to believe that the only way to be good for herself is to be good for other people and the only way to be good for other people is to forget the self. I was trying to make a saint's legend.

FULLER: When her mother contrives to humiliate Maria by getting Matthew into bed with her sister, Maria acts as if nothing has happened. What's the significance of that?

HARTLEY: She's transcended the need for revenge. Her mother's obsessive, petty, manipulative behavior is the behavior of a desperately disturbed person. Why lower herself to that level? On the other hand, why should Maria assume Matthew to be impervious to her sister's temptations? It's humility. And it takes a saint to maintain it.

FULLER: Do you think Matthew and Maria are in love at the end of the movie?

HARTLEY: I think it's charity. In its original sense, charity means the highest and most divine form of love; disinterested and seeking no reward. In that sense, yes, I think they are in love.

FULLER: Your films seem to posit love as a kind of transcendent state, but the characters share a kind of knowledge that it's a route fraught with danger.

HARTLEY: Oh, absolutely. At the end of *The Unbelievable*

Truth, love may enable Josh and Audry to transcend all the bullshit in a very physical, immediate sense, but it doesn't make life any easier or any less dangerous. And then with *Trust* I wanted a love story that didn't gloss over the more difficult implications of commitment and intimacy.

FULLER: Do you think your films are about escape? Both Audry, in *The Unbelievable Truth*, and Maria, in *Trust*, want to break away. Even your early short film, *Kid*, is about the desire to leave.

HARTLEY: That was my senior film in college and it is a discussion about wanting to escape. The whole experience of going to college, which was a great experience for me, was about forming dependencies and having to break them; dependencies on ways of thinking and on certain teachers. By the time I came to make my graduation film, I knew that it had to be about forging my own identity, trying to be very deterministic and saying, "The world is going to be like this because I want it to be like this." But I realized that this was crazy. Myself and the world are only the result of what has happened before. So *Kid* was about escape, but it was also about the pointlessness of trying to escape. It's not really escape that's important – what's important is recognizing what I'm trying to escape from and who I am.

Trust is about Maria coming to grips with the fact that she can escape, and the fact that what she has to do is make decisions – which is not necessarily escaping – and take responsibility for her own life. In *The Unbelievable Truth*, Audry is someone just too young, too weak, too disappointed, to do anything but be depressed by the state of things. But simply by falling in love, by being engaged in a very personal and direct situation, experiencing a crisis, she begins to have more of a sense of herself as an individual instead of a slab of meat in a world she feels may end at any time. She begins to act. She begins to see that, "Yeah, maybe the world will blow up, but I can't stop living. That's not going to help."

FULLER: It's kind of alarming at the end of *The Unbelievable Truth* that Audry "hears the bombs" again in her head.

HARTLEY: It should be alarming. Audry is too pessimistic and Josh too optimistic. They kind of trade. He gives her some of his optimism and she gives him some of her skepticism. And at the end, sure, she's happy. She has changed. She is able to fall in love, for instance, in a world she suspects may be ultimately doomed, but she is *not* going to turn a blind eye to it as it is. Even now, after the Cold War, it's an extremely dangerous time. It's naive to assume atomic bombs won't destroy the world.

    I really like the Audry character. I remember writing Audry and shaking with excitement, saying, "This is somebody I like, who is all fucked up, definitely, but maybe not all that fucked up." It was so easy, once I got an image in my head of who she was, to have those words come out of her mouth.

FULLER: Audry and Josh have a shared interest in George Washington. Where did that motif come from?

HARTLEY: Just prior to *The Unbelievable Truth*, I had been writing a script in which this guy who runs a machine shop meets the ghosts of Benjamin Franklin and George Washington. He keeps meeting the fathers of his country on the street, or in bookstores, or in libraries, or in McDonald's. But that story was going nowhere. The juxtaposition of what George Washington popularly represents with this story of emotional commerce seemed appropriate for *The Unbelievable Truth*.

FULLER: The characters in *Simple Men* have a much stronger arc than those in *The Unbelievable Truth* and *Trust*.

HARTLEY: Certainly the film has a much more recognizable point of beginning and conclusion. It's not exactly complete closure, but Bill basically comes back to Kate and is willing to be taken away in chains, which is kind of a variation on the end of *Trust*. *Trust*'s ending, in a way, was much more complex because Matthew and Maria didn't decide exactly what that ending would be. They decided how they were going to do things, but then the

world at large came in and ended the movie. In *Simple Men*, the ending is the result of Bill's decision.

FULLER: At the end of each successive movie, you seem to move an inch closer to a resolution. Excepting *Surviving Desire*, the couples seem to be getting closer to forming a relationship.

HARTLEY: It's true. *Surviving Desire* was definitely not about the closure, or completeness, of a relationship that's formed. Instead, it's about a relationship blowing apart. A relationship built entirely on the wrong foundations. But I think the Jude character reached an understanding of himself, of his place in the world. It's a little sadder for Sofie somehow. I feel that she hasn't yet recognized the small tragedy that has happened, and that's really what I wanted to end with. She's not a bad person. She's not evil. She hasn't manipulated him in any way consciously. It's just simply that because she's young she can't see certain things. And in *my* life I just have to accept when that happens. I can kick myself all over creation forever because I made certain mistakes, but I have to accept the fact that I couldn't have known how to avoid them at the time. And I do learn by experience.

FULLER: Just after Sofie kisses Jude in *Surviving Desire*, he goes into this impromptu deadpan dance with two other guys on the street. There's also a rock band rehearsing. What were you trying to do with these scenes?

HARTLEY: I was just curious. I don't like rock videos, but I like to see dance. I like to hear music and play it. I like that live recording, that documentation, that authenticity. That has a lot to do with the dance sequence as well—the documentation of the work and concentration that goes into the execution of a simple spectacle. Here, it's men dancing. It kind of started when I was rehearsing some scenes for *Theory of Achievement*; Jeff Howard, who is an actor I work with often, came over one day with his accordion and played the song for that film. I remember thinking, "That's how easy it is to make honest cinema." Just turn the camera on and point it at somebody doing something, and they'll do all the work. They'll feel it—they

won't be pretending anything. I find that very pure and
fascinating.

When I was writing the script for *Surviving Desire*, I
devised this joke of Sofie kissing Jude and then leaving him
there, hanging. The script then goes on to say, "He
stumbles out of the bar, falls off the curb, but kind of
saves himself by doing this little shuffling dance." And
then, very unrealistically, this other man happens by and
does the same sort of funny dance step, and then they go
their separate ways. Somewhere we began talking about it
and it became more and more elaborate. It introduces
archetypal gestures that we were very conscious of: the
grabbing of the crotch (where we were deliberately quoting
Madonna, who was already quoting an existing cultural
gesture herself), the crucifixion, *West Side Story*, etc.

That dance is not disturbing particularly, but it is
very emotionally confusing. By the time they get to the
end, I feel that what started out as a lighthearted dance of
joy, because he's been kissed, is turning into a complex
expression of vague doom.

FULLER: The elation in that dance is as bitten back as all other emotions in your film. Your characters very seldom smile.

HARTLEY: It's an easy win, a smile, you know.

FULLER: You don't allow actors to emote – which is what most actors do in most other films. Even when Matthew punches somebody walking into a bar in *Trust* it's undramatic, almost contrapuntal.

HARTLEY: It's a footnote about violence.

FULLER: You forbid actors from investing the dialogue or the ideas they're putting across with any kind of emotional pitch, and this is something that goes right through your work.

HARTLEY: The thing is, none of us are really the work. The work is the work. The film is the work. I am probably as close to it as it gets, because the film is, actually, a result of my preoccupations. I don't want anybody's contribution to be so particular as to take away from the guiding aesthetic principle of the entire piece. The piece itself should have a personality. There shouldn't be disparate personalities within the piece. I guess my job, by the time I'm directing it, is one of "taste"; of determining balances, judging what seems appropriate and what doesn't. I don't like to call attention to acting, I don't like to call attention to photography. I know my films are extreme in certain ways, like the fact that nobody smiles. But I like to think that the camera work shows a similar restraint. I want the photography, the acting, the sound recording, the editing, the music, and the dialogue all to have a perfect understanding of each other, to all be working in concert.

MARTIN DONOVAN: Hal allowed me to smile a couple of times in the café scene in *Surviving Desire*.

HARTLEY: Yeah – I thought we were out of control.

FULLER: When you first worked together on *Trust*, was this something that you discussed? Were there certain qualities you wanted to bring to Matthew, or did Hal say, "Look, this is how we do it"? And did you find yourself tuning into that minimalist wavelength immediately?

DONOVAN: If you had asked me that during the making of or right after *Trust*, I don't know how I would have answered you. I obviously brought something in myself to the role in auditioning for *Trust* that Hal liked and thought was appropriate. In the reading, and then after he told me I was cast and I'd read with other people to cast the other roles, he pretty much let me alone. I don't remember major directorial stuff from Hal during that period. But when we got on the set everything changed, and it was hard to catch on to the idea that, visually, Hal wanted a very basic, simple film technique that was virtually choreographed. In terms of the character's emotional life, smiles, that sort of thing, Hal didn't say much about anything. If he said anything, he would say, "Faster." He would say, "Less," or, "Don't use your face."

HARTLEY: Ideally, by the time I get to the set, that's all my direction is: technical. Sometimes I have people going over the top, but they've got to use the appropriate gestures. That's one of the things I think I made a lot of headway on with particular actors in *Simple Men*. I felt like this is the result of four years of steady working with actors I know. When it came down to it, we could use the same terminology on the set to describe appropriate actions and gestures for what is best going to convey an emotional moment. I find it very entertaining when the characters say exactly what a scene seems to be about, but then move on to bigger things. Why try to give an impression of an idea? Why try to illustrate it? Words already exist to express it perfectly. But the words can serve as a foundation for the reality of gestures; gestures which attempt to express things more "unspeakable." And words can be gestures too.

What I want the actors to do is not to pretend – just *do it*. Our rehearsal time is an attempt to isolate and specify the appropriate gestures of expression. It's this physical expression that the actors fill up with their understanding of their characters. These physical gestures need to be understood and believed in. And this tends to eliminate pretense. It seems like a blunt, easy way to do it, but it's actually very difficult.

DONOVAN: When you're in a relationship with a director that's working there is air pressure. You feel something coming from the director and you feel something coming out of you and it keeps you in balance. As an actor, it has to do with knowing that the director is paying attention to what you're doing, and that that person is there for you. The more I work, the more I want a strong director, who gives me tasks, tells me what to do.

HARTLEY: Pressure is a really good image. Because–as a director–if you're not getting any pressure from an actor, there's not a whole lot you can do. You've got to have a force. You've got to have a shape to work against.

FULLER: Is it harder to work with Hal, where you have to rein yourself in, as opposed to directors who might want some flamboyance?

DONOVAN: If you'd asked when we were making *Trust*, I would have said yes. I would have said, "It's the most difficult thing, it's horrible, I don't like it, Hal's a tyrant." Now I realize I like it much more than working with a director who doesn't have ideas. But that doesn't make it easier.

HARTLEY: The only usable word in the whole process is "appropriate." When it seems inappropriate, I know I'm missing the point.

FULLER: Your films are about real people experiencing real emotions. People do express anger in your films, for example, but there is no hysteria. In life, people do get hysterical . . .

HARTLEY: But hysteria is sloppy and art can't be sloppy. In art, you get the chance to do it right. Every moment in my film should be as important as any other, whether it's a pause or whether it's a word. I appreciate precision in art.

FULLER: You've been compared to Harold Pinter and David Mamet, because there's a similar stylized accent on the words in your films.

HARTLEY: I'm flattered by the comparison, though I don't really know a whole lot about either of them. Their work is primarily in theater. Specificity is something I like about Mamet's movie *House of Games*. It's also why I like Bresson. He doesn't waste time on things that don't convey meaning. Every single frame of his films conveys meaning,

even if it's an image of someone sitting with nothing to
say. Everything Bresson shows you says something. I
figure that's what film does best—convey those moments of
meaning in action.

FULLER: Do you feel you're groping for certain philosophical
truths in the making of each film, specifically through what
the characters are experiencing?

HARTLEY: All my films are a desperate attempt to make some
philosophic sense out of my own experience. I want to
know more. And what the characters go through are little
exercises, little experiments; the most effective means with
which to make the world and my own experiences
understandable to myself.

FULLER: Is it therapeutic, do you think?

HARTLEY: No. If you define "therapeutic" as something you
hope is going to make you better able to deal with life,
then no. I'm not entirely sure making films doesn't simply
complicate my life. I don't need therapy—I don't think.
But then, what do I know? If I can use it now, I could've
used it ten years ago. I have the same problems now as I
did when I was answering phones for a living. Things may
be different now. I have more money and it's easier to
meet women now that I have my picture in the paper, and
being published with my scripts and all. But the
fundamental problems of my life are still the same.

　　This is all to say that I don't think making films, for
me, is therapeutic. But I do think that it is still a process
of grappling with philosophical issues every day, which I
still have to do whether I need therapy or not. I think it's
absolutely necessary. Anybody can live philosophically. I
can pack boxes in a department store and still live
philosophically. And I might be happy that way.

FULLER: This relates to the male protagonists in your features.
In *The Unbelievable Truth*, Josh is a car mechanic; in
Trust, Matthew is an electronics whiz; in *Simple Men*, Bill
fixes motorbikes. These skills are somehow ennobling.

HARTLEY: To Josh in *The Unbelievable Truth*, the simple
usefulness of fixing cars, the concreteness of it, is
consoling. In this, he has a lot in common with Maria in

Trust. Likewise, Matthew's insistence on the adequate maintenance of machinery is a kind of respect, an affirmation of human ingenuity. For all his antisocial behavior, his respect for a "well made thing" is a real gesture of hope.

FULLER: It's redemptive, isn't it, doing things?

HARTLEY: Yes, especially when it's useful. But Josh's priestly skill for fixing cars becomes a commodity and a marketing chip in his love, and this cheapens everything.

In *Simple Men* I was interested in these two brothers: Dennis, a student with few practical skills, and Bill, a man of concrete action. He can fix motorcycles and rob banks, and has all the confidence that comes along with that. I wanted to juxtapose the usefulness of the contemplative life with the life of action. People are attractive when they do what they like and they do it well. You like to be around them. When your car is broken down and you don't know what to do, the first man or woman who comes along and knows how to fix it is suddenly your savior and you want to buy them a drink. You just want to sit down and talk to them. I've always found that to be true. As superficial as it sounds, that actually might be the root of my interest in these skills. As in real life, I have never really been interested in people who are wavering, who don't know what they like, who don't know what they value. *Simple Men* is about some very confused people, but people who still have real strong convictions or feelings and have developed concrete skills based on those convictions.

FULLER: There are Oedipal relationships in all your films, but particularly in *Simple Men*, where Dennis is sexually attracted to his father's girlfriend. I wondered if you've read Freud?

HARTLEY: I've read as much Freud as any college student has read Freud, but not much more. I guess that incident in *Simple Men* denotes an awareness of Freudian analysis. I don't want to take credit for knowing more than I do. But I guess Freudians would have fun, too, with the fact that Maria winds up wearing Matthew's mother's dress in *Trust*. That was very calculated and very prepared.

FULLER: What about *The Unbelievable Truth*, in which Audry's father has a repressed sexual desire for her?

HARTLEY: That was really the whole motor for that story. I had seen a middle-aged construction worker on the subway one evening gazing at a *Penthouse* magazine. I found myself watching this man and asking myself, "I wonder what would happen if his daughter were the girl in the centerfold? What would he think about that?" That's where it started. I wanted to know where those *Penthouse* girls really came from. What did their moms and dads think about the way in which they made their living? This line of questioning led to a lot of other things.

FULLER: There is little concession to sensuality in your films, or at least to titillating the audience.

HARTLEY: I think my films are very sensual, but you're right, they're not titillating. I'm the first person to say that films are about sex. But I'm bored by seeing other people fuck. I probably resent it. Movies, though, are great about flirtation, about *trying* to get laid. When I see the standard sex scene in a movie I have otherwise been enjoying, I feel like I am viewing a tire gone suddenly flat. Everything that was compelling is gone. I like foreplay. I am much more interested in the *mechanics* of what leads to consummation. A movie should never consummate. I think sometimes that I've avoided explicit sex in my movies because it's embarrassing. It's redundant. Redundancy is embarrassing. And, of course, it always seems beside the point. I don't have any questions to ask about fucking. Whereas I have a lot of questions to ask about the more mundane aspects of life. Attraction, flirtation, disappointment, affection, resentment, contempt—these things make my head spin.

FULLER: Is it the same with violence? As well as that undercurrent of sex in your films, there's an undercurrent of violence.

HARTLEY: I am much easier with people slapping each other, punching each other. It's a different kind of flirting. They rarely ever break out into fighting.

FULLER: Women slapping men in the face is a regular occurrence in a Hal Hartley film—again in *Simple Men*.

HARTLEY: I like the immediacy of a slap. It can be used to mean anything, but at the same time a slap is so specific. I try to treat a slap or a shove in the same way I treat a puff on a cigarette or the delivery of a line. It's almost as if it's expressive because it's so generic. People falling down — I love people falling down. I've always got my eye out for flat spaces to have someone fall down on. Empty highways have this almost narcotic attraction for me.

One day, I'd love to make a film that is entirely constructed of, say, fifteen gestures. These absurd, admittedly arbitrary gestures give a skeleton to which the actor's intelligence applies itself. The best acting I've seen has always been under extreme technical constraints, because that's when you see the actor really working and paying attention, thinking the feelings. The camera has no conscience, it has no psychology, it has no philosophy, it has no history, and no expectations. The camera simply records execution — and the execution becomes expression. That's what I'm trying to get at with small things like Jude's hand almost touching Sofie's hand in *Surviving Desire*. I suspect that this concentration on physical gesture is ultimately where the expression of emotion lies.

FULLER: In *Simple Men*, characters talk about Madonna. That interested me because there aren't that many references to pop culture in your movies.

HARTLEY: There will be more of that. *Simple Men*, I think, is where that begins.

FULLER: The reason I bring it up is because your films have a certain timeless quality.

HARTLEY: But the way to make a film timeless is to time it. In college, my literature professor, Bob Stein, said, "The thing all classics have in common is that they speak *about* their time, but speak *to* all time. I learned that from Godard too. For example, he subtitled *A Married Woman*, "Fragments of a Film Made in 1964." In effect it conveys that "this is a film made now, by a person like me, in these circumstances." You can watch it thirty years later and say, "Look at what they were wearing then," and that becomes part of the appreciation of the piece. Godard, in a way, *addressed* the fact that women wore miniskirts in the sixties. In *Don Quixote*, Cervantes addressed the fact that he was writing at a particular time at the end of a generation of Romance literature and "the way I'm telling you this story has a lot to do with the time in which it was written." I was brought up thinking an artist should strive to make his work timeless. I'm trying to be an artist, so I'm trying to be timeless. I'm trying to date my films appropriately. It's only inappropriately dated films that become ridiculous and don't say anything about their time and about eternity.

FULLER: Do you think your films are inherently political?

HARTLEY: They're probably consequently political. I don't know if trying to speak about the human condition as honestly as possible *is* a political thing. I know it can be, I know it can be used politically. But it's not my primary intention.

FULLER: In *Trust*, Matthew's decision to quit his job at a factory where they are knowingly manufacturing faulty computers is a political—or at least a moral—principle.

HARTLEY: I think so. It's about dissatisfaction with certain aspects of society. Having a guy grab his boss's head and put it in a vice instead of a meek, mild-mannered guy who doesn't say anything must display an appreciation for a particular moral certitude. But is that necessarily political?

FULLER: In *Simple Men*, you revive the character of Ned from *Kid*. Is that something you'd like to experiment with further?

HARTLEY: Actually, Vic Hugo [Audry's father] and Mike [Josh's fellow mechanic] from *The Unbelievable Truth* are in *Simple Men*, as the same characters. They are the same actors playing the same characters in a different situation, with references to their past lives in the other movie. I was encouraged to use one actor in more than one role in *The Unbelievable Truth* by watching Lindsey Anderson's *O Lucky Man!* Continuing to do it from film to film is an attempt to elicit this feeling of a curiously small world.

FULLER: You shot *Simple Men* in Texas. How did you make it look like a Long Island coastal suburb?

HARTLEY: It was very easy. Long Island looks like most other places. It's flat and nondescript. We avoided photographing indigenous vegetation. And also, whatever was red, that Texan brownish red, we painted white. We put fish up everywhere.

FULLER: Are you going to shift away from your Long Island locales?

HARTLEY: The Long Island era is *done*. I started to make films in Long Island because that was the only place I *could* make films. You don't want to be in a vulnerable position when you're making a film. You always go back to a neighborhood where you know you have the possibility of controlling the environment. As a filmmaker, that's one of the first things I learned. I always knew I could do that back home in Lindenhurst, so it just became kind of logical to write scenes that took place there. Why write a scene that takes place in Sweden when you know you're going to have to shoot it in Lindenhurst?

FULLER: Audiences are naturally going to conclude that you're saying something about that environment.

HARTLEY: *The Unbelievable Truth* and *Trust* are set in variations of the archetypal American suburb: one is safe and pretty, and the other is more menacing and cold. The whole country is covered with suburbs like these. Lindenhurst was incidental. *Simple Men,* which was shot in Texas, is the only film I've made with Long Island being integral.

Simple Men actually takes the topography of Long Island into question. Bill and Dennis are somewhere like in New Jersey or New York City and they have to get out to the end of Long Island—which is an island that stretches away from the mainland and ends in one of two points. If you're afraid of being trapped, don't run to the corners; in this case, Montauk Point. There's only the ocean. There's either a boat waiting for you or you're fucked. I always thought that was kind of interesting, this idea of running away to a definite end.

FULLER: You've used epigrams like "Knowing is not enough" in *Surviving Desire,* and "There's only trouble and desire"

xxxviii

in *Simple Men*. At what point did they suggest themselves to you?

HARTLEY: In my thinking process, when I'm trying to make sense of something, I tend to think things through to a point where there are one or two or three little slogans or phrases that somehow retain more meaning than all the thoughts I've had up to that point. It's an organizing principle at first. But then I start using them in situations because they force the characters to make distinctions. They force distinctions on the situations. I think, maybe, that's why there are slogans and clichés. They don't come around by accident—they come around because they appear to be appropriate. This is not always a good thing, but it's something I can't ignore about human nature. The thing about propaganda, for instance, is that it tries to force black and white explanations on complex realities.

FULLER: Are you trying to create a perfect film?

HARTLEY: I can't imagine going out to make a film and not having an idea of what a perfect film is. But it changes. When I made *The Unbelievable Truth* I thought I knew what a perfect film was. But it's different now. It always is.

FULLER: Now that you've finished *Simple Men*, what are your feelings about the film? Has it taken any unexpected twists and turns as you've edited it?

HARTLEY: All the films do. It's always much easier to talk about what a film might mean a year or two after I've made it. But the excitement I feel right now about *Simple Men* is the excitement of discovering, gradually, over the past three months of editing, that what I thought the film was is not what the film is. I always thought that the film was significantly different from *The Unbelievable Truth* and *Trust*. Maybe not in temperament, but in subject matter. But it's not, really. There's something about the end, of Kate refusing to lie, and Bill coming back to her and giving himself up to the police. It's like there is no escape from inequity. One way or the other, he's got to pay. I'm beginning to see that that's a very consistent world outlook for me. You don't get something for nothing, *ever*.

xxxix

FULLER: Is there much of a difference between the script and the finished film?

HARTLEY: There are a few scenes I totally rewrote, based on the character of the actors I worked with. Karen Sillas, who plays Kate, is an actress I went to college with, and she was in a few of my short films. I hadn't seen her in a long time. I had been thinking of someone else in the role of Kate and was writing it that way. At the last moment, I got Karen. There is now something particularly formidable about the character and, by the same token, a peculiar weak spot in her, which I hadn't written into the script. She's very lonely. Much more lonely than I had thought. Karen brought all this in with her.

FULLER: Does the film say what you wanted it to say, or has that changed too?

HARTLEY: It says much more than I anticipated it saying. Sometimes I think a scene is going to be about one thing and I try to make it as moving as possible, but then I begin to see that its real meaning is something I didn't necessarily write.

FULLER: Can you give me an example?

HARTLEY: The last moment of *Simple Men*, which I was very excited about when I was writing it. It felt really appropriate. It felt poetic. It felt as though I had written it with clarity and meaning. In the original script, Bill gets out of the car, throws off the cops, and leans against Kate as the Sheriff asks, "Kate, do you know this man?" Then she answers, "Yes, I know this man." End of story.

I can't paraphrase the number of things that this seemed to mean. But I thought Kate having the last word like that was what the whole movie was about. But that's not in the film anymore. When I got to that point in the editing it seemed beside the point. Now, he gets out of the car, throws off the cops, and stands before her, with everybody watching. Nobody says anything. Finally, he leans his head on her shoulder and she accepts him back. The Sheriff then says "Don't move." I can't say exactly what this means either. But it feels right. It seems necessary. Unavoidable, even.

FULLER: Did you shoot the scene with the original lines?

HARTLEY: Yeah.

FULLER: And did you shoot the scene without the lines?

HARTLEY: Well, I cut the lines out. I didn't shoot it without the lines. I cut it the way it was originally written, then had to cut things away to make it work. I had to have a little humility and say, "All right, that's beautiful, but irrelevant. Get it out."

Whenever I'm doing anything, the material I'm working with tells me certain things about what is appropriate. By the time I get all the footage back from the shoot, it's like starting from zero again. In a way, the first couple of cuts of the film are just awful, because I haven't flushed out all of my preconceptions yet. I have to imagine I'd just found all this stuff in an attic, and I'm going to try and make meaning out of it.

FULLER: The key principle of your work seems to be that paring down.

HARTLEY: Essential. That's a word I like to use a lot. Finding the essential.

Simple Men

Simple Men was first shown as part of the Official Competition at the Cannes Film Festival on May 11, 1992. The cast includes:

BILL MCCABE	Robert Burke
DENNIS MCCABE	Bill Sage
KATE	Karen Sillas
ELINA	Elina Lowensohn
MARTIN	Martin Donovan
MIKE	M. C. Bailey
VIC	Christopher Cooke
NED RIFLE	Jeffrey Howard
KIM	Holly Marie Combs
JACK	Joe Stevens
SHERIFF	Damian Young
MOM	Marietta Marich
DAD	John MacKay
MARY	Bethany Wright
SECURITY GUARD	Richard Reyes
FRANK	James Hansen Prince
VERA	Mary McKenzie
Cinematographer	Michael Spiller
Production Designer	Dan Ouellette
Editor	Steve Hamilton
Music	Ned Rifle
Executive Producers	Jerome Brownstein
	Bruce Weiss
Producers	Ted Hope
	Hal Hartley
Written and Directed by	Hal Hartley

EXT. LOADING DOCK. EARLY MORNING.

VERA *is a sexy twenty-three-year-old with a gun aimed at the security guard's head. The* SECURITY GUARD *dares not move. He is blindfolded.*
Behind them we see FRANK *and* BILL *loading a truck with boxes of high-tech computer equipment.*
VERA: (*Ferocious*) Don't move!
GUARD: OK.
VERA: Did you just move!
GUARD: My foot's asleep.
VERA: I said don't move!
> (*Then* BILL MCCABE *walks over. Of the three, he seems to be the boss criminal. He grabs Vera's gun, takes her by the chin, and kisses her passionately on the mouth. She melts.*
> *The* GUARD *doesn't move.*
> *Then . . .*)
BILL: Alright, good-lookin', get in the truck.
VERA: But, Bill . . .
BILL: Come on. I'm right behind you. Come on, Frank, what are you waiting for?

3

(She starts to go, but stops and looks back at him. She runs back into his arms and they kiss again. Then . . .)
What's wrong?

VERA: Do you love me?

BILL: Yes.

VERA: Am I beautiful?

BILL: Yes, you're beautiful.

(She moves off and approaches the truck.
BILL is confident, smooth, and handsome. He thrusts the gun in his pocket and glances over at the GUARD as he lights a cigarette and oversees the last of the loading. To GUARD.)
Don't move.

GUARD: OK.

(BILL seems satisfied with this crime. He takes a hit off a flask of scotch he has with him and offers some to the GUARD.)

BILL: You want a drink?

GUARD: No thanks.

BILL: You sure?

GUARD: I'm not allowed to drink on the job.

(BILL sees the GUARD is wearing a little Catholic medallion bearing the image of the Virgin Mary. It strikes his fancy. He moves closer and lifts it.)

BILL: Hey, that's nice.

GUARD: It's the Virgin Mary.

BILL: She's good lookin', huh?

GUARD: She brings me good luck.

BILL: Can I have it?

GUARD: But she keeps me out of danger.

BILL: You're not in danger.

GUARD: Is that true?

BILL: Sure, it's true. My gun doesn't even work.

(Convinced, the GUARD nods and lets BILL remove the medallion from around his neck. BILL puts it around his own neck.)
Thanks.

GUARD: Be good to her and she'll be good to you.

(And with that he jumps off the loading dock and heads for the truck.

4

FRANK *is standing before the truck with* VERA *close beside him. He trains his gun on* BILL.)

FRANK: Sorry, Bill. It's all over.

(BILL *stops, looks around, then takes a cautious step or two closer to* FRANK *and* VERA.)

BILL: (*Confused*) What is this?

FRANK: Vera's with me. I got ideas of my own about how to run things.

(BILL *goes white. He looks at* VERA, *but she turns away.*)

BILL: Vera?

VERA: (*Desperately*) I gotta do what I feel! I gotta be happy!

(BILL *pushes Frank's gun out of the way and approaches* VERA.)

BILL: Since when are you unhappy?

VERA: You deserve better than me, Bill!

(FRANK *comes between her and* BILL.

BILL *just looks at her, dumbfounded, then at* FRANK. *Then he looks back at* VERA.

She runs off to the truck.

And FRANK *hands him an envelope.*)

BILL: What's this?

FRANK: It's three grand.

BILL: (*Appalled*) Three grand! I put this whole thing together! I stand to make ten times this much once we deliver this stuff!

(FRANK *backs away to the truck.*

BILL *is devastated. Not knowing what to do, he turns and looks back at the blindfolded* SECURITY GUARD. *The* GUARD *speaks into the wind . . .*)

GUARD: Be good to her and she'll be good to you!

(BILL *looks weakly back at the truck just as . . .*

It pulls away and speeds up the deserted street.

BILL *is left standing there in the street, clutching the envelope. He throws it to the ground. He takes out his gun, aims at the truck, and . . .*

Click. Click. Click. It doesn't work. He drops his arm and stares dejectedly at the ground before him. Then he looks up. He hears a siren. He snatches the envelope up off the ground and runs.)

5

INT. POLICE STATION. MORNING

Bill's younger brother, DENNIS, *comes striding into the police station.*
COP: And what can I do for you, young man?
DENNIS: I believe my father is being held here.
COP: Who's your father?
DENNIS: William McCabe.
    (*The* COP *looks up, impressed.*)
COP: No shit.
DENNIS: (*Nods bashfully*) Yes sir.
    (*The* COP *leans close . . .*)
COP: Listen, kid, I saw your father play with the Dodgers back
    in 'fifty-six. No matter what else people say about him,
    good or bad, your old man was the greatest shortstop that
    ever lived.
DENNIS: Can I see him?
COP: (*Leans back*) No.
DENNIS: Why not?
COP: He had a stroke in the holding cell. They took him to
    the hospital.

6

INT. COFFEE SHOP. MEANWHILE.

BILL *enters and looks around, demoralized. He sees a young woman,* MARY, *seated at the counter. He goes over and sits down beside her. They acknowledge one another coldly.*

BILL: (*To waitress*) Coffee.

MARY: What's wrong with you?

BILL: Leave me alone.

MARY: They caught your father finally after twenty-three years.

(BILL *looks at her, nonplussed, then . . .*)

BILL: What?

MARY: Look, it's in all the papers.

(*He looks at the front page story, then hands back the paper and turns to the counter.*)

BILL: (*Weary*) Big deal.

MARY: It is a big deal. It says right here he's responsible for that bombing.

WAITRESS: (*Off*) What bombing?

MARY: His Dad. Twenty-three years ago he lobbed a bomb in the front door of the Pentagon.

BILL: That hasn't been proven yet.

7

WAITRESS: (*Off*) That's your father—William McCabe—the radical shortstop?

BILL: (*Irritated*) What about my coffee?

WAITRESS: (*Off*) The man's a hero.

BILL: My father's a crazy old man.

MARY: It says here seven people were killed and he's responsible.

BILL: And I suppose you believe everything you read, right?

MARY: Drop dead.

> (BILL *reaches into his pocket and brings out the three grand. He gives her half of it. She picks it up off the counter and looks at it, impressed.*)

BILL: Here, this oughta hold you for a good long while.

> (*She slips it into her bag and sips her coffee. Finally . . .*)

MARY: I got married.

BILL: (*Unimpressed*) Oh yeah, to who?

MARY: Him.

> (*She motions across the room and* BILL *follows her gaze. He sees a young* GUY *with a lot of tattoos playing pinball.* BILL *turns back around without comment and sips his coffee.*)

BILL: How's the kid?

MARY: (*Getting up*) OK.

BILL: (*Stops her*) That money's for *him.*

MARY: (*Icy*) Don't take your bad conscience out on me, Bill.

> (*This stings him. She moves away and exits with her* HUSBAND. *As they are exiting we see* DENNIS *passing by. He sees* MARY *and stops. She gestures inside and* DENNIS *sees* BILL. *He comes in.*)

DENNIS: Hey, what are you doing in town?

BILL: Working.

DENNIS: You hear about Dad?

BILL: Yeah.

DENNIS: He's in the hospital.

> (BILL *looks up, surprised.*)

INT. HOSPITAL. TWENTY MINUTES LATER.

BILL *and* DENNIS *come striding in through the doors to the emergency desk. Once in,* BILL *grabs* DENNIS *by the arm and freezes, going white.*

8

Six POLICEMEN *are running up the hall toward them.*
DENNIS *is confused;* BILL *is mortified.*
But the POLICEMEN *troop right on past them and out into the
street.*
BILL *relaxes and* DENNIS *leads the way to the desk.*

INT. HOSPITAL. MORNING.

At the desk: The NURSES *are all confused and excited.*
NURSE OTTO: (*Breathless*) Can I help you?
DENNIS: Yeah. We're here to see about a patient. William
　　McCabe.
　　(*All the bustling* NURSES *stop. They look at* BILL *and*
　　DENNIS. *There's a moment of awkward silence, then . . .*)
NURSE LOUISE: (*Steps forward*) Are you his family?
BILL: (*Impatient*) He's our father.
DENNIS: Is he OK?
NURSE LOUISE: I think your father's a wonderful man! I don't
　　care what the newspapers say about him!
NURSE OTTO: Go back to your station, Louise!
NURSE LOUISE: (*Being pulled away*) He wouldn't have blown
　　up that building if he knew people were in there! He's a
　　great man! Falsely accused!
NURSE OTTO: Louise!
BILL: Look, lady, can we see him or what?
NURSE OTTO: (*Turns back*) No you can't.
BILL: Why not?
NURSE OTTO: Because he's gone.
BILL: Gone where?
NURSE OTTO: He's escaped.

INT. MOM'S APARTMENT. A LITTLE LATER.

MEG MCCABE *is sitting at the kitchen table when she hears the
boys enter.*
DENNIS: Mom, what's going on?
MEG: I'm leaving, Dennis. I'm going to Florida. I'm afraid
　　your father might show up and I just don't wanna ever
　　see him again.

9

(*To* BILL.)
What are you doing in town, Bill?!
BILL: Got anything to eat?
MEG: Have you seen Mary?
BILL: (*Opens fridge*) I'm taking this bottle of scotch.
MEG: She lets that child run wild in the streets, you know.
    (DENNIS *is at the table, preoccupied.*)
DENNIS: Mom, you know where he might go?
MEG: Who?
DENNIS: Dad.

INT. LIVING ROOM.

MOM *packs to leave as* BILL *sits on the couch.*
MEG: Keep an eye on Dennis. Don't let him do anything
    stupid.
BILL: Look, take this.
    (*He takes the wad of cash out of his coat and hands it to
    her.*)
MEG: Where'd you get that?
BILL: Never mind where I got it. Will you just take it? You'll
    need it.
    (*She takes it, hesitating, then . . .*)
MEG: Is this dirty money?
BILL: All money is dirty money, Mom. Now will you shut up
    and take it before I don't wanna give it to you anymore!
    (*He stands and slams shut her suitcase.*)

INT. MOM'S KITCHEN. DAY.

In the kitchen: DENNIS *is still at the table concentrating.*
MEG: When I saw him last he made me memorize this
    telephone number. He said in case of an emergency I
    should ask for Tara.
    (*She hands him the number. He looks at it, then . . .*)
DENNIS: You don't want to call?
MEG: It's over with us, Dennis. It has been for years. (*After a
    moment, she gets up and puts on her coat.*) You should be
    back in school.

DENNIS: I still have time.

MEG: Did you get the money?

DENNIS: (*Nods evasively*) Yeah.

MEG: Good. Keep an eye on Bill. Keep him outta trouble.

DENNIS: Right.

> (*She kisses him and leaves.*
> *He listens to her leave the apartment. When the front door slams, he looks down at the number in his hand. He turns it over and sees it is a photo of* MEG *as a pretty young woman on the beach at Coney Island.*
> *He moves to the phone and dials. He waits, then . . .*)

OPERATOR: (*Off*) The number you have dialed has been disconnected.

EXT. MOM'S APT. DAY.

BILL *and* DENNIS *are sitting on the front stoop.* BILL *is looking at the phone number on the back of the photo.*

BILL: What area code is this?

DENNIS: Long Island, I think.

BILL: (*Hands back photo*) What's it mean?

DENNIS: I don't know. It might be where Dad is.

BILL: Did you try calling it?

DENNIS: It's disconnected.

BILL: You oughta walk away from this thing, Dennis. Dad's in deep shit. You oughta just go back to school.

DENNIS: I'm not going back to school.

BILL: Don't be stupid.

DENNIS: (*Adamant*) I'm not going back.

BILL: What are you gonna do then?

DENNIS: I'm gonna find Dad.

BILL: Dennis, don't do that!

DENNIS: I'm not asking you to come!

BILL: Well good! Because I'm not! I'm just telling you it's a stupid thing to do! (*Pause, then . . .*) Look, lend me a hundred bucks, will ya? I gotta get outta town.

DENNIS: I don't have any money.

BILL: Well, go to the cash machine.

DENNIS: I don't have any money in the bank.

BILL: What about your scholarship money?

DENNIS: I gave it to Mom.

BILL: (*Furious*) You gave it to Mom?!

DENNIS: Yeah. I was gonna ask you for money.

BILL: I don't have any money.

DENNIS: I've got twenty dollars, if you want that?

BILL: (*Wild*) Twenty dollars! What am I gonna do with twenty dollars!

DENNIS: Are you in trouble?

(BILL *glares at him resentfully. Then he turns away and smokes. He sits on the stoop.*)

BILL: I don't know.

DENNIS: What happened?

BILL: I robbed some computers.

DENNIS: But you didn't get caught, right?

BILL: I got double-crossed.

(*They sit in silence.* DENNIS *waits for further explanation.*)

DENNIS: So what's that mean?

BILL: I don't know what it means. I just gotta get outta town!

(*They sit there in silence again for a while, then . . .*)

DENNIS: Come with me.

BILL: Where?

DENNIS: To find Dad.

BILL: How?

DENNIS: I don't know exactly. I guess I'll try to track down this Tara.

BILL: (*Sceptical*) With twenty dollars?

DENNIS: Well, that oughta get us to Long Island, don't you think?

BILL: How should I know?

DENNIS: I've never been to Long Island.

BILL: Yes you have.

DENNIS: I have?

BILL: Yeah, you've been to Queens. Queens is Long Island.

DENNIS: Queens is part of New York City. I don't think it's really considered Long Island.

BILL: It's part of New York City, but it's *on* Long Island.

DENNIS: Queens is a borough.

BILL: A borough *on* Long Island.

DENNIS: A borough of New York City.

BILL: Right.

DENNIS: Long Island's a terminal moraine.

BILL: What?

DENNIS: Terminal moraine. It's the earth deposited by a receding glacier.

BILL: (*Stubs out cigarette*) Well shit! What the hell are we waiting for? Come on!

(*He stands and walks off.* DENNIS *follows.*)

INT. PENN STATION. LATER.

BILL *and* DENNIS *are at the ticket window.*

BILL: Yeah, um. How far out on Long Island can two people go for, say, fifteen dollars?

(*The* TELLER *browses over a chart, figures, then . . .*)

TELLER: Not far.

DENNIS: Will it get us to a 516 area code?

TELLER: Yes.

EXT. SUBURBAN TRAIN STATION. AFTERNOON.

The train leaves the station and BILL *and* DENNIS *are revealed on the lonely platform looking out over the town.* BILL *surveys the wide, flat, nondescript suburb. Then . . .*
BILL: Don't do anything suspicious, alright?
DENNIS: Like what?
BILL: You know what I mean.
    (*And he moves off.* DENNIS *hesitates, then follows.*)

EXT. STREET. MOMENTS LATER.

They come walking across the street from the station toward a closed up bar called the Station Café. The sign still hangs, weather-beaten and off-kilter, above the door.
They walk around the side and DENNIS *starts peeking in through the dusty windows. They go around back to where they hear some sort of commotion.*

EXT. BACK OF CAFÉ. SAME TIME.

NED RIFLE *is a guy about thirty years old with the words "missed opportunity" written all over his face. He is kicking the shit out of an old and broken-down motorcycle.*
BILL *and* DENNIS *watch in amazement.* NED *keeps lifting up the motorcycle and throwing it down again in the dirt. He jumps on it, spits at it, kicks it, and finally jumps down and wrestles it into submission. He punches its headlight out and stops when he sees* BILL *and* DENNIS.
They stare, dumbfounded, then also notice . . .
KIM, *a dangerously sexy thirteen-year-old in a convent school uniform and a black leather jacket. She's got a nose ring. She looks up over the newspaper she's reading and stares at the two brothers, unsettling them. They look back at* NED.
Heaving with exhaustion, he comes a few steps closer.
NED: Where'd you come from?
BILL: (*Uneasy*) New York City.
NED: Big deal.
BILL: (*Of bike*) What the hell are you doing to that machine?

(NED *doesn't answer at first. He tries to think and then just
passes his hand over his face. He attempts to form words, to
give shape to the vast and complicated situation that seems to
be tormenting him. But he fails. His wrath dissolves into
sadness.*
BILL *can hardly believe what he's witnessing. He looks at*
DENNIS, *but* DENNIS *just looks away, embarrassed.*
NED *throws himself on the ground.* KIM *gets up and, folding
her paper, walks away.* DENNIS *follows her.*
BILL *hesitates, then moves cautiously forward and kneels over*
NED.)
Listen, pal, take it easy.
NED: It's the fucking clutch assembly! It won't stay in gear!

EXT. FRONT OF CAFÉ. SAME TIME.

DENNIS *comes around the front of the building and finds* KIM
leaning against the windows. He passes her and looks in.
KIM: It's open.
DENNIS: What?
(*She enters.* DENNIS *waits, but then follows her in.*)

EXT. BACK OF CAFÉ. SAME TIME.

BILL *has lifted the bike up and is inspecting it while* NED *leans
against the café, scowling.*
BILL: Hey. What's your name?
NED: (*Slowly, reluctantly*) Ned.
BILL: (*Approaches*) Listen, Ned. How much will you pay me to
fix this motorcycle?
NED: It can't be fixed.
BILL: Yes it can.
NED: It will never run again.
BILL: Yes it will, I promise.
(NED *gets up and sits by the curb.*)
NED: There's nothing like a machine to make a man feel
insignificant.
(NED *looks across the street and sees a* NUN *having a
smoke—she moves off.*)

15

INT. CAFÉ. SAME TIME.

DENNIS *wanders through the place looking for a phone book.*
KIM: Ned's parents used to own this café.
DENNIS: (*Busy*) Oh yeah?
KIM: They're dead now.
DENNIS: I'm sorry to hear that.
KIM: They had a suicide pact.
DENNIS: (*Looks up*) What?
KIM: It was awful. Blood all over the place.
   (DENNIS *looks around at the place with a new sense of dread,
   then he shows her the phone number.*)
DENNIS: You have any idea what area this exchange might
   belong to?
   (*She drops her books and approaches.*)
KIM: (*Looks*) Eight eight four. I don't know. Let's call the
   operator. Gotta quarter?
   (*He gives her one and she moves to the phone booth. He
   follows her and stands aside as . . .
   She speaks into the phone.*)
   Hello operator. I need to know what region of Long
   Island has the exchange 884. (*She listens, then . . .*)
   Yeah, I realize it's an uncommon request, but my
   boyfriend is bleeding to death. (*She waits, then . . .*)
   Thank you.
   (*To* DENNIS.)
   She's looking it up.
   (KIM *then lets the photo of Dennis's mom drop to the floor of
   the booth.* DENNIS, *who can see it plainly, reaches in for it,
   balancing himself by placing his hand on Kim's knee.
   Meanwhile she's responding to the operator . . .*)
   Sagaponeck?
   (*The* NUN *enters and almost lights herself a cigarette. Then
   she looks over and sees . . .*
   DENNIS, *with his hand on Kim's leg above her knee and his
   face just beneath the level of her skirt, and* KIM, *seated before
   him with her legs open.* DENNIS *suddenly realizes his hand is
   touching the girl and whips it away. He stands and steps
   back.
   The* NUN *takes a step into the room.*

16

KIM *stands and takes a few steps away from the phone booth toward the* NUN, *looking around the room with a bored expression.*)

NUN: What's going on in here?

KIM: (*Coy*) Oh nothing.

(DENNIS *doesn't move. The* NUN *walks in toward him. Passing* KIM, *she hits her in the back of the head . . .*)

NUN: Get back over and get on the bus!

(KIM *runs out. The* NUN *comes right up to* DENNIS *and stares him down.*)

And who are you?

DENNIS: I'm a friend of Ned's.

NUN: You don't look familiar.

DENNIS: I'm not from around here.

NUN: I see.

EXT. BEHIND CAFÉ. MOMENTS LATER.

BILL *hides his gun as . . .*

KIM *is ushered back toward the convent school by the scowling* NUN. BILL *looks up from his work as they pass.*

KIM: (*Sotto to* BILL) Sagaponeck.

BILL: (*Confused*) Don't mention it.

(*The* NUN *shows* KIM *into the bus and scowls at* BILL *before moving off.*)

INT. CAFÉ. LATER THAT NIGHT.

Across the café, by the front windows, BILL *and* DENNIS *each take a hit off the bottle of scotch and resume their conversation. They're drunk.*

BILL: What difference does it make?

DENNIS: It would mean he's innocent.

BILL: The man's a fanatic. A dangerous fanatic; whether he's innocent or not.

DENNIS: He was a radical. That doesn't make him a fanatic. A lot of people were radical back then.

BILL: But you do agree he's a criminal?

DENNIS: Well, so are you!

17

BILL: That's different.

DENNIS: How's that different?

BILL: Dennis, the difference between Dad and me is that I've just fucked with the law and he's fucked with the government.

DENNIS: The law and the government are the same thing.

BILL: No it's not. The government doesn't have to obey the law.

DENNIS: Well, maybe that's not the way things should be.

BILL: Who wants a government that's gotta obey the law?

DENNIS: A lot of people do!

BILL: Yeah, well, that's why a lot of people aren't running the country.

(DENNIS *moves off to go to sleep in the phone booth.* BILL *follows him.*)

DENNIS: You're drunk!

BILL: Listen, Dennis, let me tell you something about the law. The law is just a contract. A contract between the rich people who own everything and the poor people who want to take it away from them. The contract says: If you break the law and you get away with it, fine. But if you break the law and get caught you gotta play by the rules and pay the price. It's no big moral thing. You don't have to have an ideology to knock over a liquor store!

DENNIS: Leave me alone.

BILL: (*All fired up*) And another thing. If we do catch up with the old man, I'm gonna give him a piece of my mind!

DENNIS: Yeah, right.

BILL: What's that supposed to mean?

DENNIS: You wouldn't last ten seconds with the old man.

BILL: Oh you don't think so, huh?

DENNIS: He'd kick your ass.

BILL: The old man's a fool. He was a great shortstop but he blew it.

DENNIS: He was dedicated to a cause.

BILL: He neglected his wife and children.

DENNIS: Well, nobody's perfect.

(BILL *moves back to his seat.*)

BILL: The old man's finished. Out of date. He's a relic.

DENNIS: Please be quiet and go to sleep!

(BILL *is too wired to even sit still. He paces, then sits again . . .*)

BILL: I can't sleep.

DENNIS: Why not?

BILL: I'm in pain.

DENNIS: (*Leans out of the phone booth*) What?

BILL: I've got a broken heart, man.

DENNIS: (*Incredulous*) Bullshit.

BILL: (*Defensive*) I do.

(DENNIS *comes over and sits with him.*)

DENNIS: What happened?

(BILL *drinks and takes a significant pause, then . . .*)

BILL: I was set up. Double-crossed. Betrayed by the woman I love.

DENNIS: Who, Mom?

BILL: No, Vera.

DENNIS: Who's Vera?

BILL: I don't want to talk about it.

DENNIS: Suit yourself.

BILL: (*Takes out his wallet*) You wanna see a picture of her?

(*He shows* DENNIS *the picture.*)

DENNIS: Wow. She's pretty.

BILL: I would've done anything for her.

DENNIS: Sorry.

BILL: I just can't understand it.

DENNIS: You'll get over it.

(BILL *begins putting the picture away in his wallet. He insists with a deadly seriousness . . .*)

BILL: No. Dennis, I will not get over it.

DENNIS: Yes, you will.

(BILL *stops and looks right at* DENNIS.)

BILL: Dennis, I love this woman.

DENNIS: You've loved other women.

(BILL *puts his wallet away.*)

BILL: Not like Vera. Vera was special.

DENNIS: Believe me, you'll get over it.

(BILL *takes another hit off the scotch and thinks. Then . . .*)

BILL: Yeah, you're right. (*Considers, then* . . .) Tomorrow.
  I'll get over it tomorrow.
DENNIS: Now go to sleep.
BILL: But I'm not gonna fall in love anymore.
DENNIS: Fine.
BILL: Women don't want you to love them!
  (DENNIS *lies down to sleep on a diner booth bench.*)
  Tomorrow. The first good-looking woman I see . . .
  I'm *not* gonna fall in love with her. That'll show her!
  (*He paces.*) Yeah. The first good-looking . . . *blonde*
  woman I see. I'm gonna make her fall in love with *me*.
  I'll do everything right. Be a little aloof at first.
  Mysterious. Seem sort of . . . thoughtful and deep. But
  possibly a bit dangerous too.
  Flatter her in little ways. But be modest myself. They all
  fall for that shit. Make her fall hopelessly in love with
  me. (*He stops, thinks, and takes a hit off the scotch,
  then* . . .) Yup. Mysterious. Thoughtful. Deep but
  modest. And then I'm gonna fuck her.
  (DENNIS *opens his eyes and slowly looks up and watches* BILL
  as he moves to his seat once again.)
  But I'm not gonna care about her. To me she's gonna be
  another piece of ass. Somebody else's little girl who I'm
  gonna treat like dirt and make her beg for it too. (*Almost
  drinks again, but* . . .) I'm just gonna use her up. Have
  my way with her. Like a little toy, a plaything.
  (*Drinks* . . .) And when I'm done I'm just gonna throw
  her away. (*He trails off and remains staring out into the
  night.*)
DENNIS (*Embarrassed*) Are you through?
  (BILL *only slowly recognizes his brother's voice and looks back
  in at him.*)
BILL: I haven't even begun yet.
DENNIS: Go to sleep.
  (*And* DENNIS *curls back up in his coat and lies down.*
  BILL *stares at nothing for a while. Then* . . .)
BILL: I can't sleep. (*Pauses, then softly* . . .) I'm in pain.

INT. CAFÉ. NEXT MORNING

DENNIS *is still sleeping.*
KIM *appears at the front door and looks in at him.* BILL *is*
nowhere to be seen. She enters.
She has a newspaper with her. She comes down beside DENNIS
and pokes him in the arm. He wakes up, befuddled, then gets his
bearings. He sees her there beside him and clears his eyes.
DENNIS: What's up?
KIM: Look. (*She hands him the newspaper.*)

EXT. BACK OF CAFÉ. NEXT MORNING.

Click. Click. NED *toys with the gun* BILL *used during the heist.*
BILL *is preparing to leave on the bike. He is preoccupied*
with . . .
A police car parked outside the convent seventy yards away.
NED: You know, I've never held a gun before.
BILL: (*Preoccupied*) Yeah, well, don't hold it too long. Listen
    you just take that to a gun shop and don't take anything
    less than a hundred and fifty bucks for it. OK?
NED: OK.

BILL: I'm gonna take these tools.

NED: (*Sees medallion*) What is that thing?

BILL: That's the Blessed Virgin, Ned.

NED: She's pretty, huh?

BILL: Not only is she pretty, but she's got a nice personality. *And* she's the mother of God.

NED: Can I keep it?

BILL: Be good to her and she'll be good to you.

NED: Thanks, Bill.

BILL: Don't mention it.

NED: I wish I could be more like you.

BILL: You don't wanna be like me.

NED: I mean, you just get up and go. You take charge of things. You're your own man.

BILL: (*Seriously*) Ned, I don't even know where I'm going.

NED: But that's what life's all about! The adventure! The not knowing!

BILL: No it isn't.

NED: I want adventure. I want romance.

(BILL *looks at him for a moment and then sighs. He places his hand on Ned's shoulder and tries to explain.*)

BILL: Ned, there is no such thing as adventure. There's no
such thing as romance. There's only trouble and desire.

NED: Trouble and desire.

BILL: That's right. And the funny thing is, when you desire
something you immediately get in trouble. And when
you're in trouble you don't desire anything at all.

NED: I see.

BILL: It's impossible.

NED: It's ironic.

BILL: It's a fucking tragedy is what it is, Ned.

(BILL *sees the* NUN *and a young, boyish* COP *come out of the
convent. The* NUN *is talking. She points to the café.*)

Listen, I gotta go.

NED: So soon?

BILL: (*Pushing bike*) Yeah.

NED: Will you be coming back?

(BILL *pushes the bike around front, always watching . . .
The* COP *and* NUN. *The* COP *looks over, then starts following
the angry* NUN *as she marches toward the café.*

BILL *curses under his breath and wheels the bike as fast as he
can.*)

BILL: That's hard to say.

NED: Let me come with you?

EXT. FRONT OF CAFÉ. SAME TIME.

BILL *muscles the bike onto the front sidewalk just as* DENNIS
comes stepping out of the café with KIM.

BILL: Come on, Dennis! Hurry up!

DENNIS: (*Of newspaper*) Look, there's a story about the
robbery!

(*But* BILL *is having a hard time starting the bike.* DENNIS
and KIM *see . . .
The* NUN *and the* COP *stop dead in their tracks, alarmed
when they see . . .*

KIM *with* DENNIS. *Nobody moves. Suddenly,* DENNIS *turns
and moves awkwardly away, stumbling as he makes for the
bike.*

23

This is enough evidence for the NUN *and* COP *to start running.*

BILL is frantic, but finally gets the bike to roll over. DENNIS *jumps on.* NED *runs along beside them, calling over the roar of the engine . . .)*

NED: I'll never forget you guys!

(And KIM *runs over and grabs* NED *by the arm and drags him toward the café.*

The COP *comes tearing around the corner just as . . .*

BILL and DENNIS *peel out and screech into the street.*

The COP *starts to run back for his car, but the* NUN *reaches him and screams to . . .*

KIM, *as the girl lets go of* NED.*)*

NUN: *(Frantic)* Kim, look out!

(NED spins to see them and stops when he sees the cop's gun drawn.)

NED: It's not loaded! Look . . .

(BOOM! He fires a shot into the air.

BILL and DENNIS *speed away up the street.*

The COP, *with the help of the* NUN, *finally wrestles the gun away from* NED.

The NUN *grabs* NED *by the hair.)*

NUN: Where did you get that weapon?

NED: There's nothing but trouble and desire.

(The COP *grabs the medallion . . .)*

COP: What's this?

NUN: It's the holy Blessed Virgin, you idiot!

(NED tries to grab it back, but can't . . .)

NED: Bill gave it to me!

NUN: *(To* COP*)* Give it back!

COP: I can't! It's evidence!

NUN: Evidence of what?

COP: I don't know!

(The NUN *punches him in the stomach and wrestles the* COP *to the ground.*

NED falls back and begins mumbling . . .)

NED: There's nothing but trouble and desire.

There's nothing but trouble and desire.

There's nothing but . . .

(BILL *and* DENNIS *careen through traffic and make for the outskirts of town* . . .
The COP *and* NUN *slug it out in the street* . . .
KIM *leans her head against the glass of the phone booth and closes her eyes* . . .
NED *continues* . . .)
 . . . trouble and desire.
There's nothing but trouble and desire.
There's nothing but trouble and desire.
There's nothing but trouble and desire.
There's nothing but trouble and desire . . .

CUT TO BLACK.

(*A few moments of silence, then* . . .)
KATE: (*Off*) He wanted me to lie for him. But I don't lie for anybody.

EXT. DAY. A FIELD.

KATE *is in a field of tall swaying grass on the east end of Long Island. She is searching through the grass for something small.*
KATE *is beautiful and blonde. She is in her early thirties and is a straightforward no-nonsense woman. She has her back to her friend,* ELINA, *as she speaks.*
KATE: We were standing over there by the fence. I followed him out here because he was so drunk. I was afraid he might hurt himself. It was so dark.
(*As she talks we move out across the field to where* ELINA *is also searching.* ELINA *is a younger woman, quiet and mysterious.*)
He started shooting into the air and shouting. He said he was going to kill me. Somebody must've heard the shots. The police came racing down the road here. I remember, when he heard the sirens, he threw the gun out this way. (*Pauses and thinks, then* . . .) But it might have been the other field. I can't remember.
(*She notices* ELINA *is nowhere to be seen. She stops and looks around.*
KATE *runs forward and finds* . . .

26

ELINA *lying there, tossed around by violent spasms.* KATE
falls to her knees but doesn't know what to do.)

EXT. SAME TIME. A NEARBY ROAD.

Meanwhile, BILL *and* DENNIS *are at the side of a back road
tending to the worn-out motorcycle.* BILL *sweats as he works on
the engine.* DENNIS *sits a little ways off, reading the newspaper.*

DENNIS: Six hundred and fifty thousand dollars worth of
computer equipment?

BILL: Hand me that wrench will ya?

DENNIS (*Hands it to him*) That's a lotta money.

BILL: It was a beautiful crime.

DENNIS: How did you do it?

BILL: I sent Vera up here to get a job at that corporation. This
is like three months ago. Back in Maryland, I even sent
her to computer training school. Then Frank . . . you
don't know Frank . . . Frank came up and started
driving for this particular trucking outfit . . . I set
myself up as an independent contractor selling computer
software designs . . .

DENNIS: Sounds like a tough way to make a living, Bill.

(BILL *is having a hard time with the engine.*)

BILL: Fuck!

DENNIS: I mean, who are these people? Frank? Vera? How
could you be in love with a woman and not know she's
the type of person that'll turn on you like that?

(BILL *looks up over the gas tank and thinks, then . . .*)

BILL: She was beautiful.

DENNIS: She was *that* beautiful?

BILL: Yes. Here, hold this.

(DENNIS *comes over and holds a wrench in place while* BILL
takes a vice grip to whatever it is he's doing.)

I was in love, I guess.

DENNIS: You weren't in love. You were thinking with your
prick.

(BILL *looks at him over the engine, then goes back to work.*)

BILL: What's the difference?

DENNIS: Hey, look.
> (BILL *follows Dennis's gaze and sees* . . .
> KATE *standing in the road, frazzled and out of breath.*)

EXT. FIELD. MOMENTS LATER.

KATE *comes running across the field, followed by* BILL *and*
DENNIS. *She reaches* ELINA *and stops, looking on anxiously as*
DENNIS *kneels over the unconscious figure in the grass. He listens*
for breath, checks the pulse, and so on.
BILL *stands off to the side a little, feeling useless.*
DENNIS: Seems OK. Just unconscious.
BILL: (*To* KATE) Do you live around here?
KATE: (*Cautiously*) Up the road a little.

EXT. FIELD. DAY.

Moments later: DENNIS *carries* ELINA *in his arms as he follows*
KATE *and* BILL *back across the field.*

INT. BAR & GRILL. LATER.

DENNIS *sits reading at the empty bar. He gets up and goes*
outside.

EXT. BAR & GRILL. SAME TIME.

DENNIS *comes down off the front porch and hears some activity*
around back.

EXT. GARAGE.

DENNIS *finds a fisherman,* MARTIN, *filleting fish.* DENNIS
approaches, interested in the fish guts.
MARTIN: (*Off*) Is that girl epileptic?
DENNIS: (*Looks up*) Excuse me?
MARTIN: Seems like epilepsy to me.
DENNIS: (*Realizes*) Oh. Yeah. I think so too.

28

MARTIN: I had a cousin like that. Be fine for months and then bang. Not a lot you can do about it, is there?

DENNIS: (*Of guts*) What do you do with these fish guts?

MARTIN: Fertilizer.

(*He gestures toward* KATE, *who is coming down the steps from her apartment above the bar.*)

She wants to plant trees.

INT. BAR. SAME TIME.

The place is empty and BILL *has his hand in the register. He hears* KATE *come in the back way and quickly moves away.*

She comes in. She sees BILL *and stops.*

BILL: Everything OK?

KATE: Yes.

BILL: (*Sits at bar*) So you run this place yourself, huh?

KATE: Yes.

BILL: (*He hesitates . . .*) How about a beer?

(*As she gets his beer, she is looking out into the street; always on the lookout.* BILL *looks her up and down while her back is turned. He raises his eyebrows, impressed, then looks away as she returns with the beer.*)

Thanks.

(KATE *watches him, then . . .*)

KATE: Where are you guys from?

(BILL *lowers his beer and watches her carefully, then . . .*)

BILL: Why?

KATE: I'm expecting someone and I don't know if they're coming alone or not.

BILL: We're from New York.

KATE: (*Conversationally*) On vacation?

BILL: We're looking for a place called Sagaponeck.

KATE: What's in Sagaponeck?

(*He thinks of some appropriate lie.*)

BILL: (*Drinks*) A house my father once lived in.

(KATE *watches him and nods as he looks away and drinks. She leans back off the bar and stretches her neck to look out into the road.*)

KATE: If you guys need a place to stay for a few days, there's the bungalow out back.
(BILL *lifts his beer, then* . . .)
BILL: (*Cool*) I wouldn't wanna be . . . in the way or anything.
KATE: (*Opens door*) You wouldn't be. I'd like you to stay.
(*She holds his gaze a moment longer, then goes out.*
BILL *sits there, watching her go.*)

EXT. BAR. SAME TIME.

DENNIS *is busy preparing to leave on the motorcycle.* BILL *comes out of the bar and looks off at* KATE *as she walks by.* DENNIS *follows his gaze.*
BILL: (*Of* KATE) She's pretty, huh?
(DENNIS *looks back out at* . . .
KATE *as she enters the field. She lifts a bucket of fish guts and a shovel.*)
DENNIS: Are you going to fuck her?
(BILL *shoots him a look, then lights a cigarette and replies* . . .)
BILL: Maybe.
(DENNIS *sighs and looks around, impatient.*)
DENNIS: I think we should push on.
BILL: Now?
DENNIS: Yeah.
(BILL *looks out at* KATE.)
BILL: I'm tired. I think I'm going to rest a while.
(DENNIS *is disappointed and annoyed with* BILL. *He watches* BILL *watching* KATE. *Then* . . .)
DENNIS: (*Of motorcycle*) Is this thing broken?
BILL: Yeah. It's shot.
(DENNIS *just looks away, then* . . .)
DENNIS: There's a gas station up the road a few miles down. Maybe we can get some money for it.
BILL: Good idea.
(*And* BILL *walks away toward the field to join* KATE.)

31

INT. BAR. LATER.

MARTIN *comes in and finds* DENNIS *at a table with a thin
telephone book. He is searching for the number.* MARTIN *watches
a while, then . . .*

MARTIN: What are you doing?

DENNIS: Looking for an address.

MARTIN: You know, they organize that book in alphabetical
    order.

DENNIS: Oh, I know. All I have is the phone number. I don't
    know who I'm looking for.

    (MARTIN *looks at the number, pauses, then looks back at*
    DENNIS.)

MARTIN: You gonna go through the whole goddamn book?

DENNIS: There aren't many numbers in it.

MARTIN: Let me help you.

    (*And he takes the book away from* DENNIS. *He stands at the
    bar and flips through it without looking away from* DENNIS.)

DENNIS: You work here?

MARTIN: No. I gotta charter boat down at the pier.

DENNIS: Have you known Kate long?

MARTIN: I've known her a while. Her ex-husband, Jack, he
    used to own this place. But then he got into trouble with
    the law. When she divorced him the judge gave the place
    to her.

DENNIS: Where is this guy now?

MARTIN: Jack?

DENNIS: Yeah.

MARTIN: In jail. He came back here about two years ago
    threatening to kill her or something.

DENNIS: (*Looks up*) Really?

MARTIN: Jack's nasty. I mean, he's my best friend and all, but
    shit, enough's enough.

DENNIS: What happened?

MARTIN: Somebody called the cops and they came and
    dragged him outta here. Then they found he was wanted
    for something in Pennsylvania.

DENNIS: Wow.

MARTIN: That's your brother out there?

DENNIS: Yeah.

MARTIN: Your older brother?

DENNIS: Yeah.

MARTIN: You do whatever he says, huh?

DENNIS: (*Defensive*) Well, no. Not always.

MARTIN: He looks bossy.

DENNIS: He's OK.

MARTIN: He likes Kate.

DENNIS: You think so?

MARTIN: Most men like Kate.

DENNIS: Do you?

MARTIN: Yes I do. You gotta see her in a bathing suit. But she won't have nothing to do with me.

DENNIS: She seems kind of . . . jumpy.

MARTIN: Jumpy women are great.

(DENNIS *just looks across the table at* MARTIN, *then goes back to work.*)

DENNIS: Yeah, well, I wouldn't know about that.

MARTIN: No, I guess you wouldn't.

(*He finds the number and places the book back on the table before* DENNIS.)

Here you go. See you later.

(*He goes out, leaving* DENNIS *alone.*)

INT. PAVILLION LATER.

Out back of the bar there is a roofed party area with a pool table. DENNIS *stands leaning on his pool cue, studying the table.* BILL *enters and stands there beside him, watching.*

DENNIS *glances over at him, then returns his attention to the table.*

BILL *looks on, waiting for something to happen.*

But DENNIS *just continues studying the table. After a while he shifts his weight, frowns, and chalks his pool cue.*

BILL *stands back and folds his arms, curious as to the shot* DENNIS *plans to make.*

But DENNIS *just stands and studies the table some more.*

BILL: They don't move by themselves, you know.

DENNIS: (*Ignores him, then . . .*) There's geometry involved.

(*But finally, he leans down and shoots. He sinks a few balls.*)

33

BILL: Listen. I've been thinking. You're right. Maybe we should ditch the bike somewhere. Kate says we can stay here a couple of extra days.

(DENNIS *looks up from the table, thinks a moment, then hands* BILL *the photo.* BILL *sees the address and name added and is surprised.*)

T. Mulligan? Where'd you find this?

DENNIS: The telephone book.

(BILL, *impressed, hands back the photo.*)

BILL: Maybe we can get her to take us out there.

DENNIS: Who?

BILL: Kate.

DENNIS: (*Disappointed*) Oh.

BILL: What?

DENNIS: Nothing. (*He looks at the table again, almost shoots, but then . . .*) Look, you stay here. I'll go and try to find it myself.

BILL: Don't be an idiot. It could be miles away and you don't know where you're going. Six ball — corner pocket.

DENNIS: *That's* a stupid shot. It's easy to make, but it won't leave me anywhere. Look, Bill, you can have sex with every woman between here and New York City, but it's not gonna make you feel any better about Vera.

BILL: How do you know?

DENNIS: We're supposed to be out here trying to find the old man and you're running around trying to get laid!

BILL: We're supposed to be *what*? No, *you're* the one who's out here trying to find the old man. I couldn't give a shit!

DENNIS: Then why the hell have you come all this way then?

BILL: Because you asked me to!

DENNIS: Because you had nowhere else to go.

BILL: Look, I'm out here because Mom told me to keep an eye on you.

DENNIS: Bullshit!

BILL: It's true.

(DENNIS *puts down his pool cue and makes for the door in a huff.*)

DENNIS: Look, I'm moving on!

(*But* BILL *reaches out, grabs him by the collar, and swings*

him back into the room. DENNIS *falls against the pool table,
and before he can get up again* BILL *pins him by his throat.*)
BILL: Gimme that address!
   (DENNIS *gives it to him.* BILL *lets him go.* DENNIS *waits,
   still afraid, keeping his eye on* BILL.
   BILL *finds his jacket on a chair. He moves to the door, but
   stops. He feels bad, but doesn't want to apologize.*)
   Look, go take care of the motorcycle. Will ya?
DENNIS: Fuck you, I'm wanna play pool.
BILL: (*Furious*) You don't play pool! You shoot pool!!

KATE'S CAR. A LITTLE LATER

KATE *and* BILL *are driving past farmland.*
KATE: What's Dennis study at school?
BILL: Philosophy. (*Of farms.*) What do they grow out here
   anyway?
KATE: Those are potatoes.
BILL: Really?
KATE: It used to be all potato and duck farms out this way
   years ago. It used to be famous for that.
BILL: For ducks?
KATE: (*Smiles*) Yeah, ducks.
BILL: Ducks are funny animals.
KATE: I think the hockey team is called the Ducks.
BILL: They have a hockey team?
KATE: Yeah. I think so. The Long Island Ducks. I don't know,
   maybe it's soccer. I'm from Pittsburgh, myself.
BILL: Long Island's a terminal moraine.
KATE: It's a what?
BILL: It's the dirt dumped by a glacier when it melts.
   (*She watches him sceptically.*)

EXT. ROAD. KATE'S CAR.

On the road: KATE *and* BILL *drive by, passing a car parked by
the side of the road.*
*It is a red car. As they pass by, it moves off toward where they've
come from.*

EXT. GAS STATION. DAY.

DENNIS *comes in off the road, pushing the motorcycle. He is sweating. There is a young guy,* MIKE, *standing at the gas pumps playing "Greensleeves" on the electric guitar.*

DENNIS *waits for him to finish, then . . .*

MIKE: Bonjour, monsieur.

DENNIS: What?

MIKE: It's French.

DENNIS: Oh.

MIKE: (*Of bike*) Outta gas?

DENNIS: No. It's busted.

MIKE: Qu'est-ce qui ne va pas?

   (DENNIS *thinks for a second, then . . .*)

DENNIS: You mean, what's wrong with it?

MIKE: You parlez-vous francais?

DENNIS: Un peu.

MIKE: Excuse me?

DENNIS: Just a little.

MIKE: Far out, man. (*And he shakes Dennis's hand.* DENNIS *resumes . . .*)

DENNIS: As far as I can tell, the clutch assembly is shot.

MIKE: You'd have to leave it for a couple of days.

DENNIS: I was thinking you might want to buy it. Cheap. For parts.

MIKE: We'd have to talk to the boss about that.

DENNIS: Is he here now?

MIKE: No. He's getting divorced. He won't be back till later.

   (DENNIS *looks back out at the road, then returns to* MIKE *. . .*)

DENNIS: Can I leave it here and come back when he returns?

MIKE: C'est entendu.

   (*And he underlines this with a wailing little lick on the guitar.*)

EXT. ROAD IN SAGAPONECK. AFTERNOON.

KATE *pulls the car to the side of the road and cuts the engine. She and* BILL *look out at what used to be the address.* BILL *eventually gets out and looks over the car at . . .*

36

The rubble of a burnt down house. Only the foundation remains.
He comes around the car and KATE *joins him as he approaches*
the ruins. He casts a glance at the charred mailbox and checks the
address. (This is it.) He moves on.
KATE *watches as he moves comfortably amidst the blackened*
rubble and starts poking around like some sort of inspector.

KATE: I hate fire.

BILL: Don't worry about this.

KATE: When I look at something like this, I can't help but
    wonder if there were people sleeping when it happened.

BILL: No. I'm sure no one was hurt.

KATE: Really? How do you know?

BILL: This was a professional job.

KATE: What do you mean?

BILL: It looks to me like an insurance scam.

KATE: Really? You think so?

BILL: Yeah, you can tell by looking at the type of damage
    what sort've fire it was. (*Looks at the rubble . . .*) Yeah,
    this . . . this was an easy nobody-gets-hurt professional
    insurance scam.

KATE: Seems you know a lot about all this.

BILL: I used to do it for a living.

KATE: You were in the insurance business?
    (*He looks at her askance.*)

BILL: Well, yeah, sort of.

EXT. BAR. A LITTLE LATER.

DENNIS *comes walking back up the road and sees . . .*
ELINA *standing on the porch watching him.*

DENNIS: Hi.

ELINA: (*Foreign accent*) Hello.

DENNIS: Wanna cigarette?

ELINA: Where is everyone?

DENNIS: Bill left with Kate. They'll be back soon, though.

ELINA: Bill who?

DENNIS: My brother.

ELINA: And who are you?

DENNIS: I'm Dennis.

(He offers his hand but she just looks away. Then . . .)
ELINA: My name is Elina.
DENNIS: How are you feeling?
ELINA: I'm feeling fine.
DENNIS: We met up the road. You had a . . .
ELINA: Yes.
DENNIS: I carried you back here.
ELINA: Thank you.
DENNIS: It's OK.
ELINA: It's epilepsy.
DENNIS: I thought so.
ELINA: Come inside.
    (And they go inside.)

EXT. BURNT DOWN HOUSE.

KATE: I think you should know about my husband.
    (BILL *freezes, then . . .*)
BILL: Husband?
KATE: Ex-husband. He was released from prison a few days
    ago.
BILL: Prison, huh?

KATE: I just thought I should say something. I mean, to be perfectly honest, I'm a little nervous about being alone at the place right now. That's why I invited you to stay.
(*He considers all this, then . . .*)
BILL: Does he live around here?
KATE: No. He called yesterday from someplace in Pennsylvania.
BILL: What do I need to know?
KATE: Just that I appreciate your company.
BILL: And you and him, you don't get along very well, huh?
KATE: No, we don't.
BILL: What's he like?
KATE: He's psychotic.

INT. BAR. MOMENTS LATER.

ELINA *stands silently watching* DENNIS *who is sitting.*
Finally . . .
DENNIS: Do you live here?
ELINA: No.
DENNIS: Just visiting?
ELINA: Not really.
DENNIS: I see.
(*She joins him at the table.*)
ELINA: What about you?
DENNIS: What about me?
ELINA: What are you doing here?
DENNIS: I'm just passing through.
ELINA: That's pretty vague.
DENNIS: What kind of accent is that?
ELINA: Why?
DENNIS: No reason.
ELINA: Romanian.
(*She hears a car approaching and stands to look. She sees something in the road and jumps down to the floor.*)
Get down! Get down!
(*He gets down. They press themselves against the wall beside the bar as . . .*
OUTSIDE: *Through the screen door we see . . .*

The red car slowly pulls into the dirt parking lot. The
DRIVER *gets out but we don't see him. He comes up to the*
front door and stops. All we see is his hand on the window
He turns and leaves.
ELINA *and* DENNIS *gradually begin breathing again. She gets*
up.
DENNIS, *uninformed and confused, raises himself up slowly*
and approaches the bar.)

DENNIS: (*Finally*) What the hell's going on around here?
(*And she slaps him. His beer goes flying.* ELINA *steps away,*
seething.)

ELINA: Go away from here! You're going to ruin everything!
Why have you come?
(DENNIS *is stunned. He holds his face and looks at her,*
speechless. She suddenly feels confused and guilty and runs
out of the room.
DENNIS *just stands there, holding his face, amazed.*)

EXT. BURNT DOWN HOUSE. DAY.

KATE: So tell me about yourself.
(*He looks at her and smiles. He tries to think of what to say,*
but then . . .)

BILL: Oh, there's nothing to tell.

KATE: That sounds mysterious.
(*This bothers* BILL, *reminding him of his speech the night*
before. He stops and looks at her.)

BILL: (*Honestly*) I don't mean to sound that way.

KATE: You seem like a man with a lot of experience.

BILL: Do I?

KATE: Yes.

BILL: How?

KATE: Somehow very thoughtful, deep.

BILL: Do you have a cigarette?

KATE: No, I don't smoke.

BILL: I'm not deep and it's not that I'm so very thoughtful
either, it's just, you know, I'm tired.

KATE: You're being modest.
(BILL *almost shouts. But he contains himself.*)

41

BILL: I think we should be heading back.
KATE: Are you through here?
BILL: Yeah, I'm all finished.
(*And he starts to lead her away, but . . .*
She spots something at the edge of the property.
He follows her over to . . .
A small tree.)
KATE: I want to dig up this tree.
BILL: Why?
KATE: I want to transplant it.

INT. GAS STATION/BODY SHOP. THAT AFTERNOON.

MIKE *is sitting there in the cluttered office, practicing French.*
MIKE: (*Reading*) "Est-ce que les nanas sont intéressantes? Are
     the broads interesting? Oui, ce sont les nanas
     intéressantes. Yes, the broads are interesting."
     (*Then Mike's boss,* VIC, *comes in. He's always in a bad*
     mood.)
VIC: Do I pay you to sit around and talk French all day?
MIKE: Is it a black chair? Oui, c'est une chaise noire.
VIC: Move over!
     (MIKE *makes room for* VIC *to pass.*)
MIKE: How'd it go?
VIC: I'm a free man, but I'm broke. What the hell are you
     learning French for anyway?
MIKE: It's a beautiful language.
VIC: Yeah, well, so's Navaho!
MIKE: I've gotta date with that French check-out girl at the
     Deli-Mart.
VIC: She ain't French!
MIKE: Sure she is.
VIC: She is not. She's Italian.
MIKE: No way!
VIC: She is.
MIKE: (*Throws down the book*) Fuck!
VIC: What's that motorcycle doing out there?
MIKE: Some guy brought it in here earlier. He wants to sell it
     to us.

42

VIC: Does it run?

MIKE: It needs a new clutch assembly.

VIC: Who was this guy anyway?

MIKE: I'd never seen him before.

VIC: Did he have the registration for it?

MIKE: I didn't ask.

(VIC *is immediately suspicious. He walks out and looks the bike over, then comes back in.*)

VIC: He didn't leave a phone number or anything?

MIKE: Non, monsieur.

VIC: You idiot, that motorcycle could be stolen for all we know!

MIKE: I don't think this guy was a thief.

VIC: Why not?

MIKE: He didn't look like a thief.

VIC: What was he like?

MIKE: Well, he spoke French.

(VIC *rolls his eyes back and holds his head. Then . . .*)

VIC: Call in the license plate number and make sure it hasn't been reported as stolen.

MIKE: Oui, monsieur.

VIC: And stop that!

MIKE: Relax.

EXT. BURNT HOUSE. A LITTLE LATER.

KATE *is carefully digging up the tree.* BILL *stands by, waiting for something to do.*

BILL: Can I do anything?

KATE: (*Digging*) No.

BILL: You know a lot about trees, huh?

KATE: No more than anybody else, I suppose. It's really just a hobby.

BILL: You know, I was reading something somewhere, something about how—something about, you know, how, uh, trees are important.

KATE: Yeah, I guess they are.

BILL: They help the atmosphere.

KATE: They help replenish the ozone layer.

BILL: That's it! The "ozone layer."

KATE: Can you spread that piece of burlap on the ground over here, please.

(BILL *takes a three-foot square piece of burlap and spreads it out on the ground near the tree.* KATE *puts down the shovel and steps down into the little ditch she's made around the tree. She carefully but forcefully lifts the tree. Small roots snap as she pulls it out of the ground and places it, finally, onto the burlap.*)

BILL: I guess it's not good to cut down too many trees, huh?

KATE: No, I guess not. I'm no scientist or anything. It just relaxes me to work with them.

(*She stands.*)

BILL: That's what I need, a hobby.

KATE: It keeps me busy and I like that.

(BILL *grabs her and kisses her on the mouth. It's a long, smooth, well-handled kiss.*

He leans back.

KATE *is stunned.*

BILL *holds her gaze, himself breathless and amazed.*

CRACK! She slaps him and stomps angrily back to the car.

BILL *picks himself up, holding his face, shocked and confused.*

KATE *closes the trunk, gets in the car, and slams the door.*

She points out at BILL, *furious.*)

I didn't do one thing to make you think you could do that!

(BILL *stands there, amazed.*

KATE *starts the car, heaves a sigh, then looks back out at him.*)

Are you coming or what?

(*He hesitates, but then lowers his hand from his face and cautiously approaches the car.*)

EXT. ROAD/GAS STATION. MOMENTS LATER.

KATE *goes whizzing by at top angry speed.*

EXT. GAS STATION. DAY.

MIKE *is taking money from a young* WOMAN *customer in a car with a friend.*
MIKE: Merci, madame.
> (*The young* WOMEN *giggle appreciatively as they drive away and* MIKE *grins mischievously as he pockets the money and walks over to . . .*
> VIC *and the* SHERIFF. *The* SHERIFF *is another tortured and confused man with a drinking problem and a disastrous love life. He is continually preoccupied.*)

SHERIFF: Yeah. That's it. That's the motorcycle we're looking for.
VIC: (*To* MIKE) See! What did I tell ya!
> (*The* SHERIFF *wanders back to his car . . .*)

SHERIFF: If the guy comes back here, try to detain him.
VIC: Detain him?
SHERIFF: Yeah.
VIC: How?
SHERIFF I don't know! Offer him a cup of coffee or something.
VIC: And then what?
> (*The* SHERIFF *stops and turns, irritated.*)

SHERIFF: Then, you know, call me! I'll come and arrest him, I guess!
VIC: And in the meantime this French sociopath stabs me and Mike to death!
MIKE: Fuck that, man!
> (*The* SHERIFF *flies off the handle.*)

SHERIFF: Oh, you want my job?
VIC: No, we don't want your job! We just want a little protection!
> (*The* SHERIFF *falls back in disbelief, lighting himself a cigarette.*)

SHERIFF: Protection!
VIC: Yeah!
> (*The* SHERIFF *throws his hat to the ground.*)

SHERIFF: Protection! Certainty! Assurance! Security!
VIC: (*Lost*) Well, yeah. That too, I guess.
SHERIFF: (*In a fit*) You want confidence! A pledge! Safety! Guarantee! Promises! Expectation! Consideration!

Sincerity! Selflessness! Intimacy. Attraction. Gentleness.
Understanding. An understanding without words.
Dependence without resentment. (*Begins trailing off.*)
Affection . . . To belong . . . Possession . . . Loss.
(*He stops finally and collapses. He sits on the cement base of
the gas pumps and hangs his head. VIC looks on in horror.
MIKE approaches and lays a hand on the man's shoulder.*)
MIKE: Hey, Sheriff, everything OK at home?
SHERIFF: (*Weakly*) Why do women exist?
    (*MIKE pats him on the back, comfortingly.*)

EXT. BAR. SAME TIME.

DENNIS *is sitting on the porch steps, deep in troubled thought.*
KATE *drives up and skids to a stop in the parking lot. She and*
BILL *get out, slam doors, glare at each other, go their separate
ways, etc. . . .*
KATE *goes inside and lets the screen door slam shut as* BILL *comes
up onto the porch.*
DENNIS *waits, then . . .*
DENNIS: Well?

46

BILL: Give me my cigarettes. There's nothing there.

DENNIS: What do you mean?

BILL: (*Hands back photo*) Whatever *was* there was burnt right down to the ground. *Recently.* Nothing left but ashes.

(DENNIS *is disappointed. He looks at the address sadly, then up at* BILL.

BILL *is edgy, he comes over and sits beside* DENNIS.)

You know what's going on here, don't you?

DENNIS: (*Not sure*) I guess.

BILL: We're being set up.

DENNIS: What?

BILL: These two . . . Kate and the other one . . . they're . . . (*Leans close.*) Lesbian lovers.

(DENNIS *is nonplussed.*)

Yeah, that's it. Don't you see? I can't believe I didn't see it sooner. And her *husband*, who's a psychopath, is on his way back here right now and he's probably plenty pissed off! (*And then adds . . .*) And I don't blame 'im. (*Smokes, then . . .*) That's why she wants us to hang around, you see. To give the impression, you know, that there's nothing . . . unnatural going on around here!

(DENNIS *is still staring at* BILL, *confused.* BILL *becomes irritated . . .*)

Well, say something!

DENNIS: (*Thinks, then . . .*) What do you want me to say?

BILL: Tell me I'm right!

DENNIS: I don't know if you're right.

(KATE *leans out the screen door, no longer angry . . .*)

KATE: Would you like to eat with us?

(BILL *doesn't respond. He just stares off at the road.* DENNIS *looks back at her and nods politely . . .*)

DENNIS: Yes, thank you. Can we give you a hand with anything?

KATE: (*Reenters*) No, thank you.

(DENNIS *watches her go, then looks back at* BILL.)

EXT. PAVILLION. LATER

DENNIS: I don't know if she prefers women or not, but Elina's definitely involved.

47

BILL: Who's Elina?
DENNIS: The girl. The other one.
BILL: What the hell kind of name is Elina?
DENNIS: (*Significantly*) Romanian.
BILL: Romanian?
DENNIS: Weird, huh?
BILL: Why's it weird?
DENNIS: Well, have you ever met a Romanian?
BILL: No.
DENNIS: I think she's involved.
BILL: With what?
DENNIS: With Dad.
BILL: Dennis, pull yourself together.
DENNIS: She slapped me.
BILL: Who slapped you?
DENNIS: Elina.
BILL: Elina slapped you?
DENNIS: Yeah.
BILL: What did you do to her?
DENNIS: I didn't do anything to her!
BILL: You didn't try to kiss her?
DENNIS: (*Confused*) No! Why would I do that?

BILL: I don't know, she's kinda cute.

(DENNIS *looks back at the house, remembering.*)

DENNIS: Look, that's not the point. She slapped me because she knows who we are. And she's afraid we're gonna lead the cops to Dad.

BILL: She told you this?

DENNIS: No. But it seems pretty clear to me.

BILL: Dennis, just because a girl slaps you for making a pass at her doesn't mean she's a member of some terrorist organization.

DENNIS: I didn't make a pass at her!

BILL: Dennis, the only clue you have to Dad is a burnt down house. Give it up. He's gone. Either that or he went up in smoke with the house.

DENNIS: There's more, though. Somebody drove up in a car and looked around the place.

BILL: Was it the police?

DENNIS: I couldn't see who it was.

BILL: Did they see you?

DENNIS: No. We were hiding.

BILL: You and Elina were hiding?

DENNIS: Yeah.

BILL: What was she hiding for?

DENNIS: (*Exasperated*) That's what I'm trying to tell you! She was hiding for some reason, and I think it's because she's involved somehow with Dad!

(BILL *paces a little, thinking. He looks back at* DENNIS, *very serious.*)

BILL: Look, if it was the cops, they're probably looking for me, not Dad.

DENNIS: I didn't think of that.

(*They stand there in silence for a while, then . . .*)

BILL: Come on, let's go eat.

INT. BAR. EVENING.

The place is empty. No business. KATE *and* ELINA *sit at separate tables while* BILL *and* DENNIS *sit at another. Everyone eats in silence. Finally . . .*

DENNIS: Not much business here, is there?

KATE: (*Amiably*) It's the end of the season.

DENNIS: (*Nods*) I see. (*Looks to* ELINA, *considering, then back to* KATE . . .) This is good food.

BILL: (*Impatient*) Will you shut up and eat!

(DENNIS *swings back around and continues eating.* KATE *looks on, annoyed with* BILL.)

KATE: Elina, you can sleep on the couch upstairs tonight if you want. Bill and Dennis are going to spend the night in the bungalow.

ELINA: Thank you. That will be fine.

(DENNIS *keeps eating, but* BILL *happens to look up and comes eye to eye with* KATE *as she gets up and leaves the room.*

ELINA *gets up and goes outside. She reappears behind* BILL *and* DENNIS, *listening at the window.*)

BILL: What do you say, wanna go?

DENNIS: (*Surprised*) No.

BILL: (*Urgently*) I think we should split. Right away.

DENNIS: I want to talk to Elina. Find out what she knows.

(BILL *pushes his plate away and leans on the table, deep in troubled thought.*)

BILL: I'm afraid of what went down back there with Ned.

DENNIS: Well, then it's better that you stay here, isn't it?

BILL: This isn't a good place for me to stay.

DENNIS: Why not?

(BILL *glances over toward the kitchen where* KATE *can be seen through the door.*)

BILL: Because if I don't leave right now, I might not leave.

(DENNIS *looks back over his shoulder at the kitchen, then returns to* BILL.)

DENNIS: I thought you said she was a lesbian?

BILL: (*Shrugs*) I was pissed off. I lost my head.

(DENNIS *pauses, watching* BILL. *Then* . . .)

DENNIS: I think she likes you.

BILL: You do?

DENNIS: Definitely.

(BILL *just sighs and looks at his hands.* DENNIS *waits a moment, then goes outside after* ELINA.)

50

EXT. BAR. SAME TIME.

DENNIS *comes out and* ELINA *ducks into a tool shed. He passes by her and walks out to the garage.*
ELINA *comes out and checks to see if he's gone. She climbs the stairs to Kate's living quarters.* DENNIS *comes back around from the garage and hears* ELINA *enter the apartment.*
He hurries up after her.

INT. KATE'S APARTMENT. SAME TIME.

DENNIS *searches the place and* ELINA *eludes him by hiding in the various rooms.*
Finally, he spots her and chases her into the bathroom.
She closes the door and locks herself in.

INT. BAR. SAME TIME.

BILL *lingers by the bar as* KATE *cleans up. She walks by him and he stops her. She stands there holding the dishes for a moment, then . . .*
BILL: Look, I'm sorry.
KATE: I didn't slap you because you kissed me. I slapped you because you thought I couldn't refuse.
BILL: I kissed you because I couldn't help myself.
   (*They stand there in silence, both looking around the room awkwardly. Finally, she looks back at him.*)
KATE: If you kiss me now, I promise I won't hit you.
   (*They look into one another's eyes and wait. Then . . .*
   She drops all the dishes to the floor. They rush together and kiss passionately.)

INT. KATE'S APARTMENT. SAME TIME.

DENNIS *stands outside the bathroom.*
ELINA: Leave me alone!
DENNIS: Look, I don't mean any harm. I just want to talk.
ELINA: Go talk to someone else!

51

(*He sighs and rubs his head. He walks halfway up the hall,
thinking, then comes back to the door.*)

DENNIS: Do you know who I am? (*Silence . . .*) Come on!
Answer me! Do you know who me and my brother are?
(*No answer at first. Then, quietly . . .*)

ELINA: Yes.

(DENNIS *sighs, relieved, but far from satisfied.*)

DENNIS: You know my father?

ELINA: Yes.

DENNIS: Do you know where he is?

ELINA: No.

DENNIS: Why are you afraid of me?

ELINA: I'm not afraid of you.

DENNIS: You know what I mean.

ELINA: I'm afraid you'll ruin everything.

DENNIS: Ruin what? His escape?

(*No answer.*)
You can't stay in there forever.

ELINA: (*Quietly*) Go away.

(*Exhausted and hurt,* DENNIS *gives up for now. He sighs and
walks slowly up the hall and out of the house.*)

EXT. BAR. MOMENTS LATER.

DENNIS *comes around the building and walks up onto the front
porch. But he stops when he happens to glance into the bar and
sees . . .*
BILL *helping* KATE *clean up.*

EXT. BAR/PORCH. MOMENTS LATER.

DENNIS *quietly steps back down and sits on the stoop. He sits
there silently for a time, when he suddenly realizes . . .*
ELINA *is standing at the far end of the porch.*
*He watches her as she stands there looking at him. Finally she
comes over and sits on the stoop too.*

ELINA: I think something must have happened.

DENNIS: You mean, you think something went wrong?

ELINA: I don't know. I'm only supposed to wait here.

DENNIS: For him?

ELINA: Either for him or someone else who will take me to him. (*She looks away, sadly.*) But he should have been here by now.

(*Then, to* DENNIS.)

He's done it again. He's left me behind.

(*She hangs her head, infinitely disappointed.* DENNIS *waits, respectfully, but then . . .*)

DENNIS: Excuse me for asking, but . . . are you and my father, you know, close?

ELINA: Yes.

DENNIS: How close?

ELINA: Very close.

DENNIS: You mean, you're his girlfriend?

(*She gets really defensive.*)

ELINA: Have you got something to say about that?

DENNIS: Just that the man's nearly seventy years old.

ELINA: You and your brother both put together will never be the man your father is!

DENNIS: Well, maybe not. (*He gets up and paces, then . . .*) Listen, you've got to help me to see him.

ELINA: Please don't ask me to do that.

DENNIS: I won't ruin anything. I just want to talk to him.

ELINA: It's too late for that. (*Looks down, hopelessly . . .*) And besides, he's probably gone.

DENNIS: (*Comes closer*) What was supposed to happen?

ELINA: When?

DENNIS: When he got here.

ELINA: We were going to leave the country.

DENNIS: How?

ELINA: I don't know. At first I thought you must be the person who would take me to Bill.

DENNIS: You call my father Bill?

ELINA: Well, what am I supposed to call him?

DENNIS: Even my mother calls him William.

(ELINA *jumps up, runs into the parking lot and throws herself on the ground with a sob.*

DENNIS *gets up, terribly ashamed of himself, and rushes over to her.*)

Listen, I didn't mean anything by that. I'm sorry. Really.

ELINA: (*Distraught*) He's not coming! I know it! He's left me behind! I know he has!

DENNIS: Oh, hey, come on! He wouldn't do that! He'll be here. He will.

(*She looks up at him.*)

ELINA: How do you know! You don't even know the man!

DENNIS: I know he's a man of his word. I know he believes in things!

(*She watches him a moment, then sits up and collects herself, staring at the ground.*)

ELINA: He's a womanizer.

DENNIS: (*Reluctantly*) Yeah, well, he wouldn't leave a woman as attractive as yourself behind.

(*She looks at him, gives him the once over, then looks away.*)

ELINA: You are a womanizer too, then.

DENNIS: I'm just trying to make you feel good.

(*She looks back at him, then stands up.*)

ELINA: Thank you.

(MARTIN *comes roaring up the road in his pickup. He skids to a stop in the parking lot, hops out of the truck, falls to his knees in the dirt, and screams . . .*)

MARTIN: I CAN'T STAND THE QUIET!

INT. PAVILLION. NIGHT.

Roaring rhythmic rock and roll fills the pavillion.
Tables have been upended.
Empty beer cans and bottles of booze line the bar.
KATE, BILL, ELINA, DENNIS, *and* MARTIN *dance.*
It's hot.
Steamy.
Sloppy.
Fun.

INT. PAVILLION. LATER.

A drunken debate about Madonna and economics.
Angle: Close on KATE . . .

KATE: Madonna exploits her sexuality on her own terms.

ELINA: What does it mean to exploit your sexuality on your own terms?

BILL: It means you name the price.

KATE: Madonna is a successful business person.

MARTIN: I like old-fashioned, straight ahead rock and roll.

DENNIS: She sings OK.

(ANGLE: *Close on* ELINA . . .)

ELINA: The representation of female sexuality that she offers is of strength and self-determination.

MARTIN: I don't listen to much new popular music myself.

KATE: Love songs are usually about weakness.

BILL: You can learn a lot about love from popular music.

ELINA: Is there a difference between exploiting your own body for profit and having someone else exploit it for you?

(ANGLE: *Close on* DENNIS . . .)

DENNIS: Everyone is involved with exploitation: The person whose body it is, the salesperson, and the audience that is entertained.

BILL: The significant distinction is: Who earns more money, the exploited body or the salesperson?

KATE: And what about the audience?

DENNIS: What about them?

(ANGLE: *Close on* BILL . . .)

The nature of exploitation never improves, it only changes.

BILL: Where did you read that?

ELINA: Is it a feminist achievement for a woman to maintain such control over her own career?

MARTIN: I thought we were talking about music?

BILL: Exploitation of sexuality has achieved a new respectability because some of the women whose bodies are exploited have gained control over that exploitation.

DENNIS: They earn more money.

BILL: (*Concurring*) They call the shots.

KATE: They're not thought of as victims.

BILL: If they earn the most money, no, they probably don't think of themselves as victims either.

DENNIS: But what about the audience?

BILL: What about them?

(ANGLE: *Close on* MARTIN . . .)

MARTIN: Hendrix. Clapton. Allman Brothers. Zeppelin. Tull.
BTO. Stones. Grand Funk Railroad. James Gang. T. Rex.
MC5. Skynyrd. Lesley West. Blackmore. The Who. The
old Who. Ten Years After. Santana. Thin Lizzy.
Aerosmith. Hot fucking Tuna.

INT. PAVILLION. LATER.

It's quiet now. KATE *and* BILL *are dancing close and slow to some
old tune on the jukebox.* MARTIN *is talking to himself at the bar.*
KATE *lays her head on Bill's shoulder as they dance across the
room.*

KATE: (*Sleepy*) After a while, I'm going to plant many different
kinds of trees. Eucalyptus, Olive trees, Japanese Maples,
Mimosa . . . all different kinds of trees.

EXT. YARD. SAME TIME.

ELINA *brings* DENNIS *a glass of water.*

ELINA: You shouldn't drink so much.

DENNIS: I guess not.

ELINA: Here, drink this.

DENNIS: What is it?

ELINA: Water.

> (*He drinks a little. They sit in silence a moment, looking at one another, then* DENNIS *leans forward and kisses her. He leans back.*)
>
> You shouldn't do that.

DENNIS: Why not?

ELINA: Because I'm your father's girlfriend.

DENNIS: My father's a womanizer. He's a married man. And he stood you up.

ELINA: You have no respect for your father.

DENNIS: I don't know him. But I respect his taste in women.

ELINA: So then go make love to your mother.

INT. PAVILLION. SAME TIME.

KATE *is lying on the pool table, asleep.*

BILL *sits at the table with* MARTIN, *watching her sleep.*

BILL: Pretty woman.

MARTIN: She's got principles!

BILL: A principled pretty woman.

MARTIN: Kate ain't told a lie in her whole life.

BILL: Have you known her long?

MARTIN: For a while. I used to work with her ex-husband.

BILL: You mean the angry and dangerous psychotic ex-husband?

MARTIN: Now just hold on. Jack may be dangerous, and maybe even psychotic, but I don't think he's angry.

BILL: How long have they been divorced?

MARTIN: Why? Are you looking for a wife?

BILL: I was just wondering.

MARTIN: Two and a half years, maybe.

BILL: She been alone all that time?

MARTIN: I proposed to her.

BILL: (*Amused*) Really?

MARTIN: As soon as I knew Jack was safely behind bars, yeah. I jumped at it.

BILL: You snake.

MARTIN: She won't have nothing to do with me, though.

BILL: No, huh?

MARTIN: Sometimes I think she just don't like men.

BILL: (*Indignant*) Bullshit! She likes me.

MARTIN: (*Laughs*) Yeah, I bet all the girls like you!

BILL: (*Defensive*) What's that supposed to mean!

    (MARTIN *stands to go.*)

MARTIN: I gotta go.

BILL: No!

MARTIN: I get too emotional when I drink.

BILL: Have another beer!

MARTIN: I gotta get up early!

BILL: No you don't. Sit down.

MARTIN: (*Sits back down*) I get too emotional when I drink.

BILL: Will you have another beer?

MARTIN: (*Stands up again*) I gotta go!

BILL: Why?

MARTIN: I gotta get up early in the morning.

BILL: Martin, you're drunk!

MARTIN: And emotional.

BILL: You gotta go.

MARTIN: Why?

BILL: You gotta get up early in the morning.

MARTIN: Yeah. You're right. Here, have another drink.

BILL: No. I gotta get up early in the morning too.

MARTIN: No you don't. Sit down.

(*They drink.*)

BILL: Go on. Get outta here.

(MARTIN *slaps* BILL *on the shoulder and leaves.*
BILL *watches him go, then looks over and sees* . . .
KATE *sleeping on the pool table.*
KATE *wakes up and sits on the edge of the pool table.*)

KATE: What time is it?

BILL: It's almost morning.

KATE: I'm glad you stayed.

BILL: Is it true you've never told a lie?

KATE: No, I've told plenty of lies.

BILL: Why?

KATE: Because I thought they would make things easier.

BILL: And they didn't?

KATE: No. They made things worse.

BILL: You should probably go back to the house and get some sleep.

KATE: I want to sleep alone tonight.

BILL: (*Easily*) OK.

KATE: (*Concerned*) I don't want to lead you on.

BILL: You're not.

KATE: How long will you stay?

BILL: I'm going to spend the rest of my life here.

KATE: Really?

BILL: With you.

KATE: You seem pretty confident about that.

BILL: I am.

KATE: I hardly know you.

BILL: Oh, you'll get to know me in time. I'm gonna dig up that field and plant every tree you can name. I'll work all day and bartend at night.

(*She watches him closely.*)

KATE: You're not just trying to impress me, are you?

BILL: I know what I want when I see it.

KATE: Do you always get what you want?

BILL: Usually.

KATE: Really, everything?

BILL: Well, not always.

KATE: Life gets easier when you realize you can't have everything.

BILL: You can't?

KATE: No.

BILL: What can you have?

KATE: I think you can have what you want, or what you need. But you can't have both. Usually. Unless you're very lucky.

BILL: Or very smart.

KATE: I guess I'm not very lucky or smart.

BILL: Everything is different now.

KATE: Other men have loved me, you know.

BILL: I figured as much.

KATE: And I've loved them too.

BILL: That's only natural.

KATE: And all of those men have gone out of my life. Why do you think that is?

BILL: Because they weren't me.

KATE: And who are you?

BILL: I'm the man who is going to make you happy.

KATE: That's very romantic.

BILL: Be good to her and she'll be good to you.

KATE: Are you sure you're not just trying to seduce me?

BILL: It's you who has seduced me.

(*They lock gazes for a moment, then move together as one and kiss. Finally, she steps back and smiles.*)

KATE: We'll see.

EXT. YARD. SAME TIME.

BILL *comes out and finds* DENNIS *still sitting there.*

BILL: You OK?

DENNIS: Yeah.

BILL: Where's Elina?

DENNIS: She went to bed.

BILL: She tell you anything?

DENNIS: Plenty.

BILL: Yeah, like what?

DENNIS: She's Dad's girlfriend.

BILL: (*Incredulous*) Bullshit!

DENNIS: It's true. She loves him even though he stood her up and left her behind.

BILL: (*Comes closer*) Was he supposed to meet her?

DENNIS: Yeah.

BILL: Here?

DENNIS: Yeah.

BILL: That bastard!

(DENNIS *hears something and looks out into the dark field.*)

DENNIS: What was that?

BILL: What?

DENNIS: Listen.

(*They listen.*
Nothing.
DENNIS *looks back at* BILL.)

BILL: Listen, Dennis. I'm gonna stay here with Kate.

DENNIS: You mean, for good?

BILL: Yeah.

(DENNIS *considers this and looks out at the night.*)

DENNIS: What will you do?

BILL: I'll run this tree farm over here she wants to start.

DENNIS: A nursery.

BILL: Yeah, a nursery. (*Sips his beer, then . . .*) I'd be good at that.

DENNIS: You'll give up crime?

(BILL *gives him a sharp look, as if* DENNIS *were trying to pick a fight with him. But he can see his brother is just honestly inquisitive.* BILL *relaxes and looks away.*)

BILL: Crime isn't a way of life for me. It's a . . . knowledge. It's an intelligence about things that I've been able to . . . capitalize on. But yeah, I'll give it up.

(*Again,* DENNIS *hears something.* BILL *has heard it too. They stand still and listen. Then . . .*)

That's just the breeze.

DENNIS: I thought I heard footsteps.

64

(They listen again.
Nothing.
Finally . . .)
It's nothing, I guess.
(SLAP! Now they have definitely heard the rear kitchen door
slap shut. They freeze and stare at one another.)

INT./EXT. BAR. MOMENTS LATER.

BILL *leads the way as he and* DENNIS *creep furtively into the bar*
through the back door, listening carefully.
BILL *grabs a knife off the counter.*
DENNIS *grabs a cleaver.*
BILL *bumps into a chair and motions for* DENNIS *to be quiet.*
They continue through the bar and come out onto the front porch.
They stop and listen.
Then, BILL *sees Dennis's cleaver and takes it from him.*
BILL: Gimme that.

EXT. BACK OF BAR/YARD. MOMENTS LATER.

BILL *and* DENNIS *come around back with their weapons at the*
ready.
BILL *kicks open the gate to the yard and knocks over a bucket of*
fish guts.
BILL: Fuck! What is that?
DENNIS: It's fertilizer.
> (BILL *puts down his cleaver and takes the shovel. They begin*
> *cleaning up the mess of fish innards he has spilled.*
> *Then* KATE *opens the door and looks out at them. They stop*
> *and look up at her.)*
KATE: What happened?
BILL: We thought we heard something.
KATE: Yeah, me too.
> (*She looks around into the darkness, worried, and goes back*
> *inside.*
> BILL *and* DENNIS *drop what they're doing and follow.)*

INT. KITCHEN. MOMENTS LATER.

KATE *comes in and sits.*
KATE: It's him. I know it's him.
BILL: Don't panic. Me and Dennis will stay up till daylight.
DENNIS: Where's Elina?
KATE: She's asleep on the couch.
DENNIS: No, she's not.
   (*They see that the couch is empty and the window wide open.*)

INT. HALLWAY. MOMENTS LATER.

DENNIS *steps into the hall.*
DENNIS: It's him!
BILL: It's who?
KATE: It's Jack!
DENNIS: No, it's Dad!
KATE: Whose dad?
BILL: Our dad.
KATE: What?
   (DENNIS *approaches* KATE.)
DENNIS: Kate, what does Tara mean?
KATE: Tara?
DENNIS: T–A–R–A.
   (*She looks at the two of them, at a loss, then . . .*)
KATE: That's the name of Martin's boat.
   (DENNIS *nearly falls over. He looks at* BILL.)

EXT. KATE'S HOUSE. MOMENTS LATER.

The sky is getting light. DENNIS *gets into Kate's car;* BILL *tries to stop him.*
BILL: Dennis, just let 'em go!
DENNIS: No way! Not after I've gotten this close!
BILL: He must have known you're here and he didn't want to see you!
DENNIS: This isn't about what he wants! This is about what I want!

66

(DENNIS *takes off.*
BILL *watches him drive away, then looks back at* KATE.)

EXT. KATE'S HOUSE.

BILL *comes up the stairs to where* KATE *stands in the doorway.
They say nothing, but she goes inside and leaves the door ajar.
After a few moments,* BILL *follows her in.*

EXT. GAS STATION. MOMENTS LATER.

DENNIS *goes roaring by and passes . . .*
VIC, *who is hosing down the pavement around the gas pumps. He
stops and watches* DENNIS *disappear down the road, then drops
the hose and walks into the office.*

INT. OFFICE. SAME TIME.

VIC *enters and picks up the phone. He dials.*

EXT. DOCK. MOMENTS LATER.

It's dawn and the sky is getting bright. DENNIS *swerves off the
road, drives over a small embankment, and charges right out onto
the dock.*
ELINA *and . . .*
William McCabe (DAD) *are climbing into Martin's big old boat,
the* Tara. *They stop, look up, and watch as . . .*
DENNIS *jumps out of the car and comes striding purposefully
along the dock toward them.*
ELINA *looks at* DAD. *He looks at her and she looks down.* DAD
looks back out at DENNIS.
*He steps back up onto the dock and walks a few paces forward,
then stops and waits for* DENNIS *to reach him.*
DENNIS *is almost there, walking straight for the powerful and
handsome old man, staring him dead in the eyes the whole time.*
DAD *glares out at him and lets him approach.*
DENNIS *stops about three feet away from him. He says nothing.*

DAD *holds his son's stare with a challenging smirk.*
ELINA *steps up on to the dock and waits anxiously.*
Finally . . .
DAD: Who do you think you are?
DENNIS: I'm your son.
> (DAD *is as still and immovable as rock.* DENNIS *is not*
> *intimidated, but he looks down at his feet a second, then*
> *straight back at the old man.*
> DAD *puts out his hand.*
> DENNIS *looks at it, then reaches out to take it.*
> *They shake hands firmly, Then . . .*
> *POW!* DAD *smacks* DENNIS *in the head.*
> DENNIS *falls back.*)
DAD: (*Pointing at him*) How old are you, Dennis?
DENNIS: Twenty-three.
DAD: Keep your hands off my woman! You got that!
> (DENNIS *still has to shake his head clear before he can make*
> *sense of this. Finally, and genuinely . . .*)
DENNIS: (*Groggy*) OK.
> (DAD *steps back.*)
DAD: OK. We're even. Want some coffee?
DENNIS: Sure.
> (*When they reach her at the end of the dock,* ELINA *hauls off*
> *and slaps* DAD *in the face.*)
DAD: What!
> (*Then she changes her mind and falls against his chest,*
> *exhausted. He puts his arm around her and looks at* DENNIS.
> DENNIS *looks from his father to . . .*
> MARTIN, *who steps out of the cabin of the boat. He shoves*
> MARTIN *and* MARTIN *shoves him back.*)

INT. KATE'S APARTMENT. SAME TIME.

BILL *and* KATE *are lying together in her bed. He's asleep, but she's*
still on the alert. She gets out of the bed, careful not to wake
BILL.

EXT. KATE'S HOUSE. MOMENTS LATER.

She comes down the stairs from the apartment and sets right the bucket BILL *knocked over the night before. She then sees the red car parked in front of the bar.*

INT. BAR. MOMENTS LATER.

KATE *approaches the back door, but stops when she sees . . . Through the bar, a* MAN *sitting on the front porch. She is frightened and backs away quietly.*

INT. KATE'S APARTMENT. MOMENTS LATER.

KATE *comes in and sits on the edge of the bed. She gently wakes* BILL.
KATE: He's here.
BILL: Who is?
KATE: Jack.

EXT. HOUSE. MOMENTS LATER

BILL, *still half asleep, staggers down the stairs and kicks over the fish guts again.*

INT. BAR. MOMENTS LATER.

KATE *and* BILL *creep up to the back door and look through at . . .*
JACK, *sitting on the front porch.*
He smokes with his back to them and stares out at the road.
BILL *collects himself, silently reassures* KATE, *then comes into the bar and approaches the front door.*

EXT. FRONT PORCH. SAME TIME.

BILL *reaches the front door, pauses, then steps out onto the porch. He tries to seem imposing as he looks over at* JACK, *but he stops.*

71

He is a little surprised.

JACK *is a small man: weary, strangely intense, and with a scar across his face, but not the maniac* BILL *expected.*

JACK *doesn't acknowledge* BILL, *he just stares out at the road and smokes.*

BILL *relaxes a little. He glances back at* KATE *then steps over and sits at a safe distance from* JACK. JACK *still doesn't react.* BILL *watches him from out the corner of his eye, trying nevertheless to be a forceful presence.*

JACK *very slowly leans over to* BILL, *still with his eyes straight ahead. This alarms* BILL, *but then he leans cautiously closer to* JACK, *thinking* JACK *wants to say something. But* JACK *just sits back, having changed his mind.*

BILL *looks at him oddly, then sits back himself, becoming impatient. But then* JACK *throws down his cigarette and sighs . . .*

JACK: I just came back for my leather jacket. (*Looks at* BILL.) I'm cold.

EXT. ON THE DECK OF THE TARA.

ELINA, DENNIS, *and* MARTIN *repeat after* DAD *as he reads aloud from a book entitled* Anarchy.

DAD: "We do not know when the revolution will triumph.
   —But we know that the revolution is with us.
   —And there is no doubt that if the revolution is crushed,
   —it will be crushed because, on this occasion, we have been defeated;
   —and never because we believed it useful to compromise."

DENNIS: Listen Dad, ah . . . can we talk?

DAD: Sit still, Dennis.
   "We will have on events
   the kind of influence
   which will reflect our numerical strength
   our energy
   our intelligence
   and our intransigence.
   Even if we are defeated,
   we will have performed a worthy task.
   For human progress is measured
   by the persistence and regeneration
   of selflessness
   and a willingness
   to see beyond the limits of our own time.
   And if today we fall without compromising,
   we can be sure of victory tomorrow!"
   (*He closes the book.*)

EXT. A DIFFERENT PART OF THE BOAT. MOMENTS LATER.

DAD *sits and looks out at the water.* DENNIS *approaches.*

DENNIS: Dad, did you bomb the Pentagon?
   (DAD *looks back over his shoulder at him.*)

DAD: What?

DENNIS: You heard me. Are you responsible for that bombing in 'sixty-eight?
   (DAD *thinks before answering, eyeing* DENNIS *carefully.*)

DAD: Why do you wanna know that?

DENNIS: I need to know if my father is a premeditated murderer.

DAD: Is that why you've come looking for me?

DENNIS: Yes.

DAD: (*Chuckles*) Dennis, you impress me more and more by the minute.

DENNIS: You haven't answered my question.

DAD: No.

DENNIS: No what?

DAD: No, I didn't.

DENNIS: No, you didn't plant the bomb?

DAD: That's right.

DENNIS: Do you know who did?

DAD: No. But even if I did, I wouldn't have told.

DENNIS: So you've been in hiding all this time for nothing?

(DAD *just shrugs and looks out at the water. He pauses, then looks back* . . .)

DAD: I'm good at it.

(*He walks off.*)

EXT. ANOTHER PART OF THE BOAT.

ELINA *is tense, pacing back and forth and watching* DENNIS. DAD *waits. She stops and looks at him.*

DAD: Relax.

(*She storms off in a huff.*)

EXT. GAS STATION. TEN MINUTES LATER.

DENNIS *comes driving up the road and pulls up before the pumps. He gets out and* . . .

MIKE *comes out from the garage to meet him.*

DENNIS: Good morning.

MIKE: Bonjour.

DENNIS: So is your boss interested in buying the motorcycle?

MIKE: Not really.

DENNIS: How much will he give me?

MIKE: Not much.

DENNIS: How much?

MIKE: Fifty bucks, maybe.

DENNIS: (*Impressed*) Fifty bucks! That's plenty!

MIKE: (*Desperate*) You can get a lot more somewhere else!

(DENNIS *is moving toward the office.*)

DENNIS: Is he inside?

MIKE: Can you come back tomorrow?

DENNIS: I've got to leave today.

MIKE: Look, he's in a real bad mood.

DENNIS: Besides, I'll take half that much.

(*He enters the office.*)

INT. OFFICE. SAME TIME.

DENNIS *comes in, followed by* MIKE.

VIC *appears from behind the desk with a gun trained on* DENNIS.

DENNIS *freezes.*

VIC: Hold it right there, pal!

DENNIS: (*To* MIKE) What is this?

MIKE: Vic, you never told me you were packing a rod!

VIC: (*To* DENNIS) What have you done to Kate?

DENNIS: I haven't done anything to Kate!

VIC: That's her car out there isn't it?

DENNIS: I just borrowed it!

VIC: Yeah, right, the way you borrowed that motorcycle!

DENNIS: The motorcycle was given to us!

VIC: To *us*?

DENNIS: (*Corrects himself*) To me.

VIC: You said us.

DENNIS: I don't have to talk to you.

VIC: Shut up and sit down!

(DENNIS *sits.* VIC *puts the gun to his neck.*)

DENNIS: Go ahead and call her!

MIKE: Call who?

DENNIS: Call Kate. She'll tell you. She lent me the car.

INT. BAR. SAME TIME.

KATE *and* JACK *are sitting in the bar.* JACK *is eating breakfast.*

KATE *hears the phone ring and goes to answer it.*

75

INT. KATE'S APARTMENT. SAME TIME.

BILL, *in the bedroom, hears a car pull away and looks out the window.*

EXT. BAR. MOMENTS LATER.

KATE *and* JACK *drive away in the red car.*

INT. KATE'S APARTMENT. SAME TIME.

BILL *leans back away from the window, wondering.*

INT. GAS STATION. MOMENTS LATER.

DENNIS *watches as* JACK *and* KATE *pull up and get out of the car.*
MIKE *and* VIC *are suddenly terrified.*
MIKE: Hey, is that . . . Jack?
VIC: I hope not.
MIKE: I think it is.
    (JACK *stands by the car as* KATE *walks up to the office and enters.*
    Once in, she stops and looks at MIKE *and* VIC.)
    Is that Jack?
    (KATE *takes Vic's gun and throws it aside.*)
KATE: Go outside!
    (MIKE *and* VIC *look out at* JACK *fearfully.*)
VIC: But Kate . . .
KATE: Go on!
    (*They scurry out, scared.*
    KATE *moves over to* DENNIS.)
    Dennis, what's going on?
DENNIS: I'm not sure.
    (VIC *and* MIKE *burst back in.*)
VIC: We can't let him go, Kate. The Sheriff's on his way over.
KATE: But what has he done!
VIC: He stole that motorcycle and he was involved in some big robbery the day before yesterday! It's right here in the paper.

76

(He shows her the paper.)

KATE: Get out of here!

(They run back out. KATE turns to DENNIS.)

Is that true?

DENNIS: No.

(KATE is at a loss.)

KATE: I'm going to go get Bill.

(DENNIS looks up, urgently.)

DENNIS: No! Don't let Bill come down here.

*(This cuts straight through her. A suspicion seeps into her.
DENNIS sees this.)*

KATE: Why?

DENNIS: Just don't.

*(KATE looks away, hurt.
DENNIS stands and puts his hand on her shoulder.)*

Listen. I'm sorry about this.

(She looks up weakly.)

KATE: Can I do anything?

DENNIS: Yes.

KATE: What?

(DENNIS hesitates, then . . .)

DENNIS: Help Bill get away to Martin's boat.

KATE: I can't do that.

DENNIS: Please just do it, our father's there waiting for him.

(*She hangs her head, hopelessly, and sighs. Then . . .*)

KATE: Is your father a criminal too?

DENNIS: No. He's a baseball player.

EXT. GAS STATION. MOMENTS LATER.

KATE *and* JACK *leave in their respective cars just as the* SHERIFF *drives up.*
The SHERIFF *staggers from his squad car and bursts into the office.*

MIKE: Morning, Sheriff.

SHERIFF: Yeah, right! Get me some coffee!

INT. GAS STATION

The SHERIFF *staggers in and collapses into a chair.*

SHERIFF: Are you the suspect?

DENNIS: Yes.

SHERIFF: What's your name?

DENNIS: Dennis.

(*The* SHERIFF *lights up a cigarette and takes a deep, consoling drag. He looks out the window and shakes his head in hopelessness. Then . . .*)

SHERIFF: I don't know. I don't have anybody to blame but myself. (*Leans toward* DENNIS . . .) I mean, right from the start it was a painful and unsatisfying relationship! (DENNIS *is at a loss.*)

DENNIS: (*Carefully*) I'm sorry.

(*The* SHERIFF *falls back in his chair and sighs tragically. Finally . . .*)

SHERIFF: (*Slowly*) Life . . . is sad.

EXT. BAR. MOMENTS LATER.

KATE *pulls into the parking lot and gets out of her car as . . .*
JACK *pulls up alongside of her. He gets out, but stands there by the car with the engine still running.*

79

She comes over to him, tired and angry.

JACK: Thanks for breakfast.

KATE: It's OK.

JACK: Take care of yourself.

KATE: I will.

> (JACK *gets back in the car and she watches as he drives off up the road.*
> *Finally, she turns to enter the bar.*
> BILL *comes out onto the porch as she ascends the steps.*)

BILL: What happened?

> (*She shoves him out of the way and goes inside.* BILL *is worried. He follows her in.*)

INT. BAR. SAME TIME.

KATE *collapses at a table.*

KATE: (*Screams*) Why are all the MEN in my life CRIMINAL?

> (*This stops* BILL *dead. He pauses, then glances back out at the road. He steps a little closer.*)

BILL: Where's Dennis?

KATE: He's been arrested.

> (BILL *is shocked.*)

BILL: For what!

KATE: (*Sits up*) For your crimes, no doubt!

> (BILL *is at a loss, stunned. He sits down to think.* KATE *sits back, exhausted.*)

BILL: Kate, I was going to tell you everything.

KATE: Yeah, when?

BILL: In time.

KATE: You lied to me.

BILL: I never lied to you.

KATE: You should leave now. The cops will be here soon.

BILL: I don't want to leave.

KATE: Your father is at Martin's boat. Dennis said they'll take you with him.

BILL: Take me where?

KATE: I don't know.

> (BILL *starts to get up.*)

81

BILL: I have to go get Dennis!
   (KATE *stops him. She gets up and closes the door.*)
KATE: He said not to!
   (BILL *turns to her.*)
   He wants you to go with your father.
   (BILL *looks around the room, feeling helpless and guilty.*)
BILL: Kate, they've got nothing on me if you tell them I've
   been here for the past three days.
   (*She looks up and stares at him a moment, then turns away.*)
KATE: You want me to lie for you.
BILL: Yes.
KATE: I won't lie for you.
BILL: I thought you wanted me to stay.
KATE: I do, I really do. But I won't lie for you. I'm sorry.
   (*He looks away, resigned.*)
BILL: Don't be.

EXT. PORCH. MOMENTS LATER.

The SHERIFF *and a* DEPUTY *come up onto the porch and knock
at the door.*

82

A moment later KATE *appears at the window. She doesn't open the door.*

SHERIFF: Hello, Kate.

KATE: Hello, Sheriff.

SHERIFF: Kate, I understand you know this young man we're holding over at Vic's garage.

KATE: Yes.

SHERIFF: How long have you known him?

KATE: Since yesterday.

SHERIFF: We believe he's traveling with another man.

(KATE *doesn't respond. The* SHERIFF *waits, then . . .*)
Have you seen him with another man?

KATE: Yes.

SHERIFF: When?

KATE: Early this morning.

SHERIFF: Where?

(*Kate's gaze wanders out across nowhere and she sighs wearily. Then . . .*)

KATE: Nearby.

(*The* SHERIFF *looks at the* DEPUTY *and the* DEPUTY *just looks away and moves his hat back further on his head. The* SHERIFF *looks back at* KATE.)

SHERIFF: Can you be a little more specific?

KATE: Yes.

(*They wait, but she doesn't continue. Now the* SHERIFF *is getting irritated.*)

SHERIFF: Kate, this man we're dealing with is quite possibly a dangerous criminal.

KATE: How do you know?

SHERIFF: What do you mean, how do I know?

KATE: What is it that makes a man dangerous, anyway?

SHERIFF: Look, I'm asking the questions here, OK!

KATE: Well, I guess I don't have any choice, do I?

SHERIFF: That's right, you don't!

(*The* SHERIFF *heaves a big sigh, hitches up his trousers, and sits.*)

Now look, where exactly did you see these two men together last?

KATE: In the street.

83

SHERIFF: This street?

KATE: Yes.

SHERIFF: Do you know where this other man is now?

(KATE *steels herself and looks right at him.*)

KATE: No.

SHERIFF: Where's Jack?

KATE: He left.

SHERIFF: Where'd he go?

KATE: Florida.

SHERIFF: Has this other man gone with him?

KATE: No.

SHERIFF: Do you mind if we search the premises?

(*She pauses, then . . .*)

KATE: You'll have to get a warrant.

INT. BAR. TEN MINUTES LATER.

BILL *comes in the back door, ready but reluctant to leave.*

KATE *sits at a table, sad and quiet.*

Finally . . .

KATE: Now what?

BILL: Can I have your car keys?

(*She hesitates, but then reaches into her pocket and removes her keys. She crosses the room and hands them to him. He watches her as he takes them, but she keeps her face averted.*)

KATE: Maybe they won't come back?

BILL: They'll be back.

(*She turns to him.*)

KATE: Maybe they won't ask questions.

BILL: They'll ask questions.

(*Beaten and sad, she leans against him. They kiss.*)

EXT. PARKING LOT. MOMENTS LATER.

BILL *peels out of the parking lot, swerves out onto the pavement, and speeds away down the road.*

KATE *stands on the porch, watching him go. She looks up the road in the opposite direction and sees . . .*

The SHERIFF *approaching.*

KATE *leans back against the front of the bar. She folds her arms, looks at the floor, and waits.*
The SHERIFF *and his* DEPUTY *pull up and get out. They stomp up onto the porch and wave the warrant at* KATE. *She ignores it and lets them begin their search.*

ON THE ROAD . . .

BILL *speeds along and passes . . .*

THE GAS STATION . . .

Inside, DENNIS *watches him roar by and smiles to himself.*

BACK AT THE BAR . . .

KATE *sits silently on the porch as the* COPS *pull the place apart.*

AT THE BOAT . . .

MARTIN *and* DAD *are untying ropes and preparing to disembark when . . .*
BILL *skids to a stop at the far end of the pier.*
DAD *looks up from what he's doing and stops.*
BILL *just sits there, staring at the wheel. Then he sighs and looks out at . . .*
DAD, *as he steps up onto the pier, watching and waiting curiously.*
BILL *gets out slowly and stands by the car.*
The two men stand there, fifty yards apart, watching each other and waiting.
ELINA *comes up beside* DAD *and watches* BILL *as well.*
BILL *steps aside and runs his hand through his hair, unable to decide. He hangs his head, distraught, and sighs. Once more, he looks out at . . .*
DAD *and* ELINA, *waiting.*
But BILL *just turns and goes back to the car.*
DAD *and* ELINA *watch him drive off.*

EXT. BAR. SAME TIME.

KATE *sits on the porch steps with her knees drawn up to her chin and her arms wrapped tightly around them. She broods, staring out at the road. She's ignoring the* SHERIFF *who is sitting on the porch sermonizing.*

SHERIFF: Kate, look, I know life's just one big endless quagmire of futility, broken dreams, and smashed hopes! You're not doing yourself any good covering up for this guy! You give your heart and soul to people and they just stomp it to pieces!

(*But she has seen something approaching up the road. She lifts her head.*

In the distance, BILL *is speeding toward her.*

She lowers her knees and rises slowly from the steps.

The SHERIFF *is exhorting passionately, at this point oblivious to* KATE . . .)

Love! Affection! Consideration! These things are myths! Myths invented in a torture chamber! A torture chamber in hell!

BILL *plows ahead, closer and closer.*
KATE *wanders out toward the road, never taking her eyes from . . .*
BILL *coming nearer and nearer.*

SHERIFF: (*Off*) What can we ever really know about another person anyway! They have their own needs and wants! Their own passionate and perverse dreams! Falling in love is like sticking an ice pick in your forehead . . . But we keep doing it! We hurl ourselves into the cauldron of passion! The bottomless pit of desire . . .
(*The Sheriff's fit fades away as . . .*
KATE *stands there in the parking lot, waiting.*
BILL *comes skidding into the parking lot, with a cloud of dust and screeching of tires. He jumps from the car and throws off two* DEPUTIES *as he makes his way to* KATE.
He stops before her.
She simply waits for him to do something.
He braces himself.
She waits. Then . . .
BILL *lowers his head and lays it on her shoulder. She raises her hand and holds him to herself. She holds her cheek to his head.*
He closes his eyes.)
SHERIFF: (*Off*) Don't move.

CUT TO BLACK.

Trust

Trust was first shown at the Toronto Film Festival in September 1990. The cast includes:

MARIA COUGHLIN	Adrienne Shelly
MATTHEW SLAUGHTER	Martin Donovan
JEAN COUGHLIN	Rebecca Nelson
JIM SLAUGHTER	John MacKay
PEG COUGHLIN	Edie Falco
ANTHONY	Gary Sauer
ED	Matt Malloy
RACHEL	Suzanne Costollos
ROBERT	Jeff Howard
NURSE PAINE	Karen Sillas
DELI MAN	Tom Thon
BRUCE	M. C. Bailey
RUARK BOSS	Patricia Sullivan
JOHN COUGHLIN	Marko Hunt

Cinematographer	Michael Spiller
Production Designer	Dan Ouellette
Editor	Nick Gomez
Original Music by	Phil Reed
Executive Producer	Jerome Brownstein
Producer	Bruce Weiss
Written and directed by	Hal Hartley

INT. MARIA'S KITCHEN. MORNING.

MARIA *is a spunky, well-intentioned, but troublesome and thoughtless seventeen-year-old with big hair, supermarket clothes, and a mouthful of chewing gum. She's arguing with her father,* JOHN, *while she puts on her lipstick. Her mother,* JEAN, *watches.*

MARIA: Dad, gimme five dollars.

JOHN: Listen to me, young lady. I've had just about all I'm gonna take!

MARIA: Mom, what's he talking about? Gimme five dollars.

JEAN: *Listen* to your father when he's talking to you!

MARIA: Well, what's he talking about?

JOHN: You know damn well what I'm talking about!

JEAN: Maria, you've been thrown outta school!

MARIA: I was not thrown out. I quit. Now gimme five dollars!
      (JOHN *moves forward.*)

JOHN: You little . . .

JEAN: John, stop it!

MARIA: You wouldn't *dare.*

JOHN: If I had my way around this house, I'd . . .

JEAN: John, shut up!

JOHN: What's gonna happen to her? What is she gonna do with her life?

MARIA: I'm gonna get married.

(JOHN *and* JEAN *are surprised. They look at each other, then back at* MARIA.)

JEAN: To who?

MARIA: To Anthony.

JOHN: Oh, terrific!

JEAN: Maria, don't be silly. Anthony's going to college.

MARIA: (*Lighting a cigarette*) Only to play football. When he gets out, he'll go to work with his father doing construction and he'll be pullin' in a really bitchin' salary and we'll be like totally hooked . . .

JOHN: Don't smoke in the house!

MARIA: (*Blows out smoke*) And besides, he's gotta marry me. I'm gonna have a baby!

(MARIA *gets up from the table.* JOHN *snaps straight and tall and frightening, glaring at* MARIA *who stands confronting him.*)

JOHN: That's it!

MARIA: That's what?

JOHN: I will not have a goddam *tramp* living in my house!

MARIA: (*Appalled*) Mom! Did you hear what he *called* me?

(JEAN *is isolated within herself, so* MARIA *turns back to* JOHN, *furious.*)

Bastard.

JOHN: Slut.

MARIA: (*Truly shocked*) Daddy!

JOHN: Get out!

(MARIA *hauls off and slaps him hard across the face. Everything goes quiet.* JOHN *is shocked.* JEAN *is shocked.* MARIA *looks back and forth between them, worried, then proudly throws her head back.*)

MARIA: So there.

(MARIA *leaves, slamming the door behind her.* JOHN *just stares into space, mortified.* JEAN *slowly rises from the table, watching him.*)

JEAN: John?

(JOHN *falls to the floor, his hand clutching his chest.* PEG, *Maria's older sister, enters.*)

PEG: Mom, I'm home!
  (PEG *stops when she sees* JEAN *kneeling over* JOHN *on the floor. He's lying there, staring lifelessly up at the ceiling.*)
  Mom?
JEAN: John!
PEG: What happened?
  (PEG *kneels down beside her father and touches his body. She looks at* JEAN.)
  He's . . . dead.

CUT TO BLACK.

TITLE APPEARS . . . TRUST . . . *Then the titles appear over black.*

INT. RUARK COMPUTER FACTORY. DAY.

It is a clean and orderly assembly line for the fabrication of computer parts.
MATTHEW SLAUGHTER *is working along the line. He is an absolutely possessed young man of thirty. His face is always twisted into an impatient scowl, his fists are always clenched, and he stalks wildly from bench to bench, overseeing the work. He stops and knocks over an empty carton.* MATTHEW *approaches one of the benches. A* WORKER *backs away, scared as* MATTHEW *looks down at a particular portion of an exposed circuit board. There's a cigarette gripped in the edge of his mouth and his hair is totally unkempt. This is one mean, abusive, but dedicated human being. Matthew's superior,* ED, *comes rushing over. He's all excited and itching for a fight. He's a jerk.*
ED: Slaughter! What'd I tell you about smoking on the premises?
MATTHEW: Lay off, Ed!
ED: What's this vice doing here?
MATTHEW: Drop dead. Hand me those pliers.
ED: What's this?
MATTHEW: This is a lost cause, Ed.
ED: What is?
MATTHEW: *This!*
  (MATTHEW *puts down his pliers, picks up the piece of high-*

tech machinery he's working on, and throws it to the floor. It smashes into a million pieces.
Everyone looks on, startled. ED *is outraged.*)

ED: You'll pay for that!

MATTHEW: This *crap* isn't worth the *time* we put into it!

ED: What's wrong with it?

MATTHEW: It's cheap.

ED: So?

MATTHEW: Cheap!

ED: Can't you fix it?

MATTHEW: No!

ED: Why not?

MATTHEW: (*Lights a new cigarette*) Some things shouldn't be fixed.

ED: Well, you don't have a choice, do you? The company employs you to oversee the fabrication of . . .

MATTHEW: Ed.

ED: Let me finish. The company . . .
    (MATTHEW *grabs* ED, *forces his head into the vice, and tightens it.*)

INT. RUARK COMPUTER FACTORY. DAY.

MATTHEW *takes off his lab coat, throws it to the ground, and walks away, throwing his cigarette away as he goes.*

EXT. RUARK COMPUTER FACTORY PARKING LOT. DAY.

MATTHEW *slams out a door and finds himself in the parking lot. He walks away.*

INT. HIGH SCHOOL. DAY—A LITTLE LATER.

MARIA *stands at the bottom of a flight of stairs. A group of* GUYS *in football uniform pass her on their way down. Her boyfriend,* ANTHONY, *brings up the rear.*

MARIA: Hi.

ANTHONY: (*Annoyed*) What the fuck you doing here?

MARIA: I've got to tell you something.

ANTHONY: You get tossed outta school again?

MARIA: Yeah.

ANTHONY: What the hell did you do now?

MARIA: Come upstairs.

ANTHONY: (*Obstinate*) No.

MARIA: Oh, ease up.

ANTHONY: Listen, Maria, this isn't the time to be bugging me right now, OK? I've got a game tonight, and I've gotta take my college entrance exams tomorrow . . .

MARIA: This is important.

ANTHONY: Yeah, well so's this.

MARIA: This is more important. This is more important than football.

ANTHONY: Really.

MARIA: I'm gonna have a baby.

ANTHONY: What?

MARIA: A baby, stupid.

ANTHONY: Whose baby?

MARIA: (*Hitting him*) *Yours*, you jerk!

(ANTHONY *is horrified. He walks away and collapses to the floor.*)

95

ANTHONY: How could you be so stupid?

MARIA: Oh, thanks a lot!

ANTHONY: What are my parents gonna say! I've got a scholarship on the line!

MARIA: What about me?

ANTHONY: What about you? How could you let this happen?

MARIA: I didn't just let this happen all by myself, you know!

ANTHONY: Don't try and pin the blame on me!

MARIA: I'm not blaming you! It's just that . . .

ANTHONY: You did this on purpose!

MARIA: I did not!

ANTHONY: You did this to keep me from going away to college!

MARIA: Anthony . . . You said we'd get married!

ANTHONY: What?

MARIA: You did. You said we'd get married!

ANTHONY: You think I'd marry you now? Why would I marry you now? A high school drop-out! Pregnant!

(MARIA *starts walking away.* ANTHONY *walks along beside her, screaming into her ear.*)

You know, you squeeze that brat out and you sit around watching television all day long and you know what you're gonna look like by the time you're twenty-one? Huh? Urgh! You think I need that!

(MARIA *forges ahead, but he continues harping on her* . . .)

I don't need that. These are the most important years in my life as a football player. This arm! This arm is gonna make me famous! It's gonna take me straight through college and into the NFL! And people say that I'm a smart player. They say I'm good with strategy. That's why I gotta be devoted. I wake up at six o'clock every morning and I run three miles. Then I do eighty push-ups. Then sixty sit-ups. Then I drink this mix of one raw egg, brewer's yeast, soybean extract, wheat germ . . .

(*Finally,* MARIA *can't stand it anymore and she runs off as* ANTHONY *carries on shouting.*)

EXT. MATTHEW'S STREET. DAY.

MATTHEW *walks down the street, a beer can in hand, cigarette clenched viciously in his teeth, and his eyes darting around looking for trouble.*

INT. MATTHEW'S HOUSE. DAY.

MATTHEW *closes the door behind himself.*
DAD: (*Off*) Matthew!
    (MATTHEW *starts. With the sound of his Dad's voice he becomes an intensely soft-spoken and indecisive person.*)
    Matthew! Is that you?
MATTHEW: It's me.
DAD: What?
    (MATTHEW *passes through the hall and enters the TV room.*)

INT. TV ROOM. DAY.

DAD *is some kind of retired blue-collar worker sitting on the sofa with his trucker's cap on. He wears a flannel shirt and work boots. He's big, robust, and clear-eyed. He glares at* MATTHEW.
DAD: Why aren't you at work?
MATTHEW: Well, I . . .
DAD: Speak up, for Christ's sake!
MATTHEW: I quit.
DAD: You what?
MATTHEW: I quit.
DAD: You quit?
MATTHEW: I got fired.
DAD: Well, which is it, Matthew? You quit or you got fired?
MATTHEW: (*Flustered*) It's not that simple.
DAD: Yes, it is. You quit or you got fired? Which one?
MATTHEW: I quit.
DAD: You're sure about that?
MATTHEW: Yes. I quit.
    (DAD *stands up and hits* MATTHEW *across the face.*)
DAD: You got a lot of fucking nerve, you know that? You go
    through jobs like most people go through underwear.

MATTHEW: I'll get another job!

DAD: You expect me to support you your whole goddam life, is that it?

MATTHEW: No.

DAD: What was that?

MATTHEW: I said no.

DAD: When are you gonna wake up and stand up on your own two feet, huh? You're a grown man! When I was your age I was on my own and making a damn good living!

MATTHEW: I'll move out then.

DAD: What was that?

(MATTHEW *doesn't answer.*)

Tell me what you said.

MATTHEW: You heard what I said.

DAD: Tell me what you said, coward! Come on!

MATTHEW: I said I'll move out then.

(DAD *sits down.*)

DAD: That's a joke. You wouldn't know how to take care of yourself. You oughta thank God I've been here to look after you! And when are you gonna clean that bathroom, like I asked, huh?

MATTHEW: (*Sincere*) But I did. I did it before I went to work . . .

DAD: You call that clean?

MATTHEW: Yeah . . .

DAD: Do it again!

(MATTHEW *turns and goes out.*)

You eat yet?

MATTHEW: (*Off*) I'm not hungry.

DAD: (*Shakes his head*) Fucking kid's gonna waste away.

INT. MATTHEW'S BATHROOM. DAY – A LITTLE LATER.

MATTHEW *dutifully scrubs the bathroom. The sink, the bathtub, the toilet bowl.*

INT. MATTHEW'S OWN ROOM. DAY – LATER.

Matthew's room has nothing in it except a mattress thrown on the floor, a chair by the window, and books. Hundreds of books are

scattered all over the place. He's sitting on the edge of his bed reading a book entitled Information Theory.
The door slams open and he looks up to see . . .
DAD *standing there, furious, but trying to keep calm.*
DAD: How many times have I got to tell you to clean that goddam bathroom?
MATTHEW: But . . . I . . .
DAD: Do it! *NOW!*

INT. BATHROOM. DAY – MOMENTS LATER.

MATTHEW *scrubs his heart out. With his cigarette smoking and his sleeves rolled up, he's breaking into a sweat scrubbing the toilet bowl.*

INT. CLOTHING STORE. DAY.

MARIA *sorts through clothes with a* SALESGIRL *roughly her age. She is depressed and shops with a vengeance.*
GIRL: That would look great on you.
MARIA: I like this one too.
GIRL: Try on both.
MARIA: Can I charge these on my parents' credit card?
GIRL: Sure. The dressing room is right over there.
    (MARIA *walks over and enters the dressing room.*)

INT. DRESSING ROOM. DAY.

MARIA *slips into one of the dresses. She looks at herself in the mirror and her eyes are eventually drawn to her . . .*
Stomach, which is certainly not showing any signs of pregnancy. She places her hands on her belly and tries to imagine what she'd look like pregnant.
After a moment she relaxes and slumps down into the chair behind her.
She stares at herself in the mirror. She sits there, sadly contemplating herself.

EXT. MATTHEW'S YARD. DAY

DAD *is watering the lawn. He sees . . .*
MRS. BLECH, *who is not a bad looking mom in her late thirties, having trouble starting her car.*
DAD *stops what he's doing and approaches, easy-going, good-natured, and sincerely concerned.*
DAD: What's the problem?
MRS. BLECH: Oh, I wish I knew. This damn car. It's always something.
DAD: Sounds like the battery.

INT. MATTHEW'S BATHROOM. DAY – SAME TIME.

The place is sparkling. MATTHEW *looks around to see if he's forgotten anything. He sees that he's left the sponge on the floor. He places his cigarette on the edge of the sink and bends down to get it. He tosses it in his bucket and goes out.*
BUT . . . his cigarette remains on the edge of the sink, its ash growing on and on.

INT. MATTHEW'S BROOM CLOSET. DAY.

The door swings open and MATTHEW *places the bucket on its shelf.*

INT. MATTHEW'S BATHROOM. DAY – SAME TIME.

The cigarette's ash trembles precariously and bits of it . . .
Fall down into the spotless sink.

EXT. MATTHEW'S YARD. DAY – SAME TIME.

JOEY BLECH *and his twelve-year-old sister,* GRACE, *come up to the car while* DAD *is looking into it.*
GRACE: Hi, Mr. Slaughter!
DAD: Hi, Grace. Joey, how are you?
JOEY: Fine.

100

DAD: It's nothing serious, Mrs. Blech. Just all this corrosion
here on your battery terminals.
(*To* JOEY.)
Joey, you wanna do me a favor, please? Go in the garage
there and get me a piece of sandpaper and a screwdriver,
OK?

JOEY: OK!

DAD: This won't take a minute, Mrs. Blech.

INT. MATTHEW'S BEDROOM. DAY – SAME TIME.

The voices of DAD *and the kids carry inside.* MATTHEW *is looking
thoughtfully at the floor. He reaches into the side pocket of his
jacket to get . . .*
*A hand grenade. He holds it to his chest and looks out toward the
window.*

EXT. CLINIC. DAY.

There is a group of PROTESTERS *milling around before the
entrance of a women's health clinic, carrying placards that read:
"Save our children! Close it down!"*
Across the street, NURSE PAINE *pulls up in her dented and rusting
little Pinto. She steps out of the car, tosses away her cigarette,
and regards the* PROTESTERS *with a wry, cynical shake of the
head. She's an attractive, hard-boiled, devoted social-worker type.
She sighs, slams the car door, and moves forcefully toward the
clinic.*
The PROTESTERS *see her approaching and descend upon her, wild
and righteous.*

PROTESTER 1: That's her! That's her!

PROTESTER 2: Murderer!

PROTESTER 3: Baby killer!
(NURSE PAINE *continues on through the barrage of insults
hurled at her.*)

INT. CLINIC (OFFICE). DAY.

MARIA *sits staring at the edge of the desk, childishly uncommunicative.* PAINE *watches her patiently. After a while . . .*

PAINE: What kind of questions do you have?

MARIA: I don't know.

PAINE: Do you want to have an abortion?

MARIA: I don't know.

PAINE: Do you have a boyfriend?

MARIA: No.

PAINE: Who is the father?

MARIA: There is no father.

(PAINE *holds the girl's stubborn gaze a moment.* MARIA *looks back down.* PAINE *watches her, then takes off her nurse's cap. She reaches down into her desk drawer and takes out a fifth of bourbon and two shot glasses.*

MARIA *looks on surprised, but not shocked.*)

PAINE: (*Of bourbon*) You?

MARIA: Sure.

(PAINE *pours and they drink. They sit in silence, enjoying their bourbon. Then . . .*)

You know, I'm looking at this guy, right? And I looked at him a lot before. So now I know that I've got this little piece of him actually in me. Physically *in* me. And it makes me feel completely different. I don't know, sorta special or something. And so I'm talking to him. I'm talking to him and I realize . . . I'm talking to him and I realize that he doesn't even see me. And I wonder what it was he was seeing when we did this. I go over it in my head and I know now what he's seeing. It's really simple. He's seeing my legs. He's seeing my breasts. My mouth. My ass. He's seeing my cunt. (*Looks up at* PAINE . . .) How could I have been so stupid? That's really all there is to see, isn't it?

PAINE: That's not true.

MARIA: I don't know.

PAINE: It's not true and you know that.

MARIA: I don't know anything.

INT. MATTHEW'S BEDROOM. DAY.

MATTHEW *is sitting with the grenade in his hand, smoking.*

INT. MATTHEW'S KITCHEN. DAY — MOMENTS LATER.

DAD *comes in through the door, feeling pretty good about himself.*
He opens the fridge and drinks from a quart of milk. He stands
there a moment, swallows, burps, and then remembers MATTHEW.
He listens.
Nothing.

INT. MATTHEW'S BATHROOM. DAY.

DAD *pushes open the door, looks around, enters, and stops,*
horrified, when he sees . . .
The cigarette in the sink.
The quart of milk slips from Dad's hand and . . .
Hits the floor, splashing out onto the sparkling tiles.

INT. MATTHEW'S BEDROOM. DAY.

MATTHEW, *holding the grenade to his cheek like some precious*
pet, looks up from the floor and opens his eyes. He breathes deep,
relaxed. A moment of silence, then . . .
BOOM! The door is thrown off its hinges and falls, hanging cock-
eyed to the side.
MATTHEW *slips the grenade under a book on the floor.*
DAD *is there at the door. Heaving with violence, he steps into the*
room.
MATTHEW *stands up slowly.*
DAD *closes his eyes, clenches his fists, breathes deep, and looks up*
at his son.
MATTHEW *waits.*
DAD: Who the hell do you think you are?
MATTHEW: I don't think I'm anybody.
DAD: You think you're somebody special, don't you?
MATTHEW: Just tell me what I've done wrong.
DAD: You think you shit ice-cream cones, is that it?

103

MATTHEW: All I want to do is clean the bathroom.

    (DAD *punches him in the stomach and* MATTHEW *falls to his knees, holding his gut.* DAD *goes down on his knees, face-to-face with* MATTHEW.)

DAD: I've seen your kind. I've seen 'em all my life. You just keep taking. Taking, like everything was owed to you. Like the rest of us owed you something! You're like a little child! Gimme this! Gimme that! Other people need things too, you know, Matthew! You ever think about that? You ever think about other people? You ever think about *me!*

MATTHEW: I think about you all the time.

DAD: What!

    (*No answer. He grabs* MATTHEW *by the hair* . . .)

    Did you say something?

MATTHEW: I don't know what you want!

DAD: I want . . . a little *cooperation!*

    (DAD *releases Matthew's head.* MATTHEW *stays where he is, his face to the floor.* DAD *sits on the edge of a chair, hangs his head, and sighs.*)

    I don't know. Maybe it's my fault.

MATTHEW: It's not your fault.

DAD: Well, then whose fault is it?

    (MATTHEW *doesn't answer.*)

    Huh!

    (MATTHEW *looks down.*)

    Whose fault is it, Matthew?

    (MATTHEW *is silent.*)

    If it isn't my fault, whose fault is it?

MATTHEW: (*Softly*) It's my fault.

DAD: What was that?

MATTHEW: It's *my* fault!

DAD: It's your fault.

MATTHEW: It's my *fault!*

DAD: That's real big of you, Matthew. You think that *changes* anything?

    (MATTHEW *says nothing.*)

INT. MARIA'S REAR HALLWAY. THAT AFTERNOON.

MARIA *comes in the back door and looks around for someone. She checks her face in the mirror and tries to seem cheerful.*
MARIA: Mom? Anybody home?
(MARIA *moves into the kitchen.*)

INT. MARIA'S KITCHEN. DAY – SAME TIME.

MARIA: (*Seeing people in the kitchen*) Aunt Fay? Uncle Leo? What's going on? We having a party?
(MARIA *doesn't notice that they turn away and hang their heads. She moves over to* PEG.)
Hey, Peg, we having a party? You gotta see this bitchin' top I got. Where's Mom? . . .
(PEG *moves away as* MARIA *moves into the living room . . .*)

INT. LIVING ROOM. DAY.

JEAN *is sitting on the couch, flanked by two other women. Tragedy flows from their faces, and even* MARIA *stops in her tracks, stricken.*
MARIA: (*Pales*) Mom?
(JEAN *stares, bitter beyond words.* MARIA *collapses at her mother's feet.*)
What happened? Where's Dad?
(JEAN *looks up at* MARIA.)
JEAN: He's dead.
MARIA: Dead?
JEAN: Dead. (*Slowly, cold.*) You killed him.
(MARIA *drops her head.* JEAN *grabs Maria's chin.* MARIA *stares up at her mother, amazed and frightened.* JEAN *is clear-eyed and terrifying.*)
Get outta my house.

EXT. STREETS. DAY.

MARIA *staggers blindly through the streets.*

EXT. PHONE BOOTH. DAY.

MARIA *clings desperately to the receiver.*
MARIA: (*Into phone*) Hi, Carol. It's me. How do I know?
    I . . . I didn't *mean* to! What? I don't know. Look, I
    don't have any place to go. What? Because you're my best
    friend.
    (*Click. Carol hangs up.* MARIA *looks at the receiver,
    stunned.*)

EXT. DELI. LATE AFTERNOON.

*There's a bench just outside the door of the deli. A neat and
kindly forty-year-old woman,* RACHEL, *sits at one end, watching
the traffic go by.*
MARIA *comes up and collapses on to the bench. She sits staring at
her feet, dejected.*
RACHEL *looks over at* MARIA. *She grows concerned and leans over
carefully.*
RACHEL: Excuse me . . . Maybe it's none of my business,
    but . . . Are you all right?
    (*No response.*)
    I only ask because you seem a little pale. Are you hungry?
    (*Still no response.*)
    Has something happened? Are you hurt?
    (*Suddenly,* MARIA *breaks down and falls on Rachel's chest,
    sobbing into the woman's coat.* RACHEL *is surprised and a
    little scared at first, but then puts her arm around the girl
    and holds her.*)
    Now, now. Everything will be all right. Everything will
    be OK.
    (MARIA *moves back to her side of the bench and stares at the
    ground again.*)
MARIA: That's such a *stupid* thing to say! Really stupid! How
    the hell do you know?
RACHEL: I'm sorry. It just seemed like the thing to say.
MARIA: Why say anything?
RACHEL: I don't know.
MARIA: There's nothing to say!

RACHEL: Maybe.

MARIA: Gimme five dollars.

(She looks up at the woman. RACHEL hesitates, but then reaches into her bag and hands MARIA a five-dollar bill. MARIA takes it, then looks down, ashamed. She hands it back.) I'm sorry.

RACHEL: It's OK. Go ahead. Take it. I want you to have it. *(MARIA waits a moment, then sighs and stuffs the money in her pocket. RACHEL watches her and smiles warmly.)*

MARIA: I killed my father this morning.

RACHEL: *(Not listening)* My daughter would have been just about your age.

MARIA: I didn't mean to, honest. It was an accident. We were just arguing.

RACHEL: I've spent some time in a psychiatric hospital.

MARIA: I didn't know he had a bad heart.

RACHEL: After that my husband just didn't want children.

MARIA: He always *seemed* healthy enough.

RACHEL: I wonder if deep down he blames me for her death.

MARIA: I just slapped him.

(A scrawny, bleach-blonde BIKER MOM wheels up a baby

stroller, parks it near the bench, kisses the baby, then goes into the deli, smoking a joint.)

RACHEL: I hate my husband.

MARIA: You just never know.

RACHEL: He's just like a child himself.

MARIA: How can a slap in the face kill a man?

RACHEL: He is so absurdly like a little boy. Every summer we've got to go this ridiculous resort called Cape Holiday.

MARIA: (*To* RACHEL) What?

RACHEL: I hate Cape Holiday.

MARIA: I'm sorry.

RACHEL: And our days are like clockwork. The same routine year in and year out. Him off to the city every morning with his briefcase and pipe. Then back again each evening on the five-fifteen train.

(MARIA *listens and realizes that* RACHEL *is somewhere far away in her own head. But she listens politely . . .*)

And me at home dusting a house that never gets dirty. Never gets messed up. There's no one there to mess it up. Sometimes I come home and I find myself hoping the house is a wreck. Filthy. Complete disarray. Sometimes I come home and find myself hoping the house has been destroyed by fire.

(MARIA *watches the woman oddly, waiting.* RACHEL *just stares off into space, thinking, biting her lip. The biker mom's* BABY *chortles and burps in its stroller.*

MARIA *gets up slowly, and places her hand on Rachel's arm . . .*)

MARIA: Well, thanks for the five dollars.

(RACHEL *doesn't respond. She concentrates on something unknown.* MARIA *steps away awkwardly and enters the deli.* RACHEL *snaps out of it and looks over at . . .*

The BABY *peering out at her from over the edge of the stroller. He's gripping a little plastic submachine gun.*)

INT. DELI. LATE AFTERNOON

MARIA *comes in and passes the* BIKER MOM, *who is on the pay phone.*

BIKER MOM: I don't care about any of that! What am I supposed to pay the rent with? Are you still sleeping with that slut? Yeah, well you tell her I'm gonna rip her lungs out next time I see her . . .

(MARIA *takes a six-pack out of the refrigerator and lays it on the counter. She sighs and throws down her five dollars. The* DELI MAN *is a heavy-set, pasty-faced guy in his forties.*)

DELI MAN: Let me see some proof.

MARIA: What?

DELI MAN: Come on.

MARIA: I buy beer here all the time.

DELI MAN: Not from me you don't.

MARIA: Where's the other guy? Or that lady?

DELI MAN: Look, they're not working right now. I am. If you wanna buy beer *now*, you gotta show *me* proof.

MARIA: Listen, mister. I've had a really *bad* day. Just take the money. Please.

(MARIA *pushes the money toward him. They stare each other down.* MARIA *is so worn down and wired she looks like a drug addict. The* DELI MAN *looks her up and down, thinks a moment, looks around the store, then takes the money. He puts the beer in a bag and she reaches for it, but . . . He snatches it back. She looks at him. He stares at her a moment, then motions to the back room.*)

DELI MAN: Come back here a minute.

(MARIA *doesn't move. She stares at him, edgy.*)

Come on. You want the beer?

MARIA: Yeah, I want the beer. Why do I have to go back there?

DELI MAN: I don't want you to go out the front. People might see you. They can close me down for selling you beer!

(MARIA *waits, looks around, then cautiously moves past the counter.*)

INT. DELI BACK ROOM. LATE AFTERNOON.

MARIA *enters, followed by the* DELI MAN. *She looks around and sees . . .*

MARIA: There's no back *door* here.

III

DELI MAN: (*Leers at her*) Come on, gimme a kiss.

MARIA: Oh, gross!

DELI MAN: Hey, you want the beer, you gotta gimme a kiss.

MARIA: Just gimme back the money.

DELI MAN: No way.

MARIA: Come on! That's not fair!

DELI MAN: (*Comes close*) You think it's fair you comin' in here jeopardizing my business?

MARIA: I ain't jeopardizing anything! I wanna *do* business!

DELI MAN: Right, so gimme a kiss.

MARIA: Let me outta here. You can *keep* the money.
(*She tries to get past him. He grabs her.*)

DELI MAN: I don't want the money. I want a kiss.

MARIA: You can't have both.

DELI MAN: (*Gives back money*) OK. Here's the five dollars. Now gimme a kiss. On the lips.

MARIA: Drop dead.

DELI MAN: (*Cheated*) You have to. I gave you back the five dollars!

MARIA: It was mine to begin with!

DELI MAN: Listen, you want the beer or not?

MARIA: If you don't let me go I'm gonna scream.

DELI MAN: Go ahead. My brother's the chief of police. I'll say you were stealing. They'll believe me. Not you.
(MARIA *looks at him in disbelief.*)

MARIA: Come on.

DELI MAN: (*Approaches*) Just a little kiss.
(*He moves in to kiss her. She jumps away and gets clear.*)

MARIA: Listen, I am *not* gonna kiss you. Face it.

DELI MAN: Look, I don't have to be nice about it. Now why don't you make it easy on yourself.
(*She's cornered and she knows it. She hangs her head, thinks a moment, then . . .*)

MARIA: Gimme a cigarette.

DELI MAN: If I give you a cigarette you have to take off your shirt.

MARIA: You're really disgusting.

DELI MAN: It's just business, honey. Free trade.

MARIA: Shut up and gimme a cigarette.

(*He gives her a cigarette and lights it for her.*)

DELI MAN: Take off your shirt.

MARIA: Just wait a minute, will ya!

(*He keeps pressing closer and closer . . .*)

DELI MAN: Let me see you touch yourself.

MARIA: I bet this gets you really excited, huh?

DELI MAN: (*Sweating*) It sure does! How 'bout you?

(MARIA *takes a good, long drag off her cigarette, lets him get closer, then . . .*

Sticks the cigarette in his eye . . .)

YEOWWWWW!

(*He falls back into a stack of boxes.* MARIA *picks up the beer and runs out.*)

INT. DELI. LATE AFTERNOON.

MARIA *runs through the store and out onto the sidewalk.*

EXT. DELI SIDEWALK. LATE AFTERNOON.

MARIA *slams out the door and stops dead in her tracks when she sees . . .*

The BIKER MOM *standing, horror stricken, staring down into . . .*

The empty baby stroller.

BIKER MOM: They stole my baby!

(MARIA *looks over at . . .*

The bench. RACHEL *is gone.*

The DELI MAN *stumbles out the door, howling in pain, and falls to the ground.* MARIA *runs off in a panic.*)

BIKER MOM: (*Knocking over the baby stroller*) Fuck!

EXT. STREET. LATE AFTERNOON.

MARIA *wanders aimlessly through the streets, clutching her bag of beer.*

113

EXT. ABANDONED HOUSE. NIGHT

MATTHEW *approaches a derelict house.*

INT. ABANDONED HOUSE. NIGHT.

MATTHEW *sits down, takes the hand grenade out of his pocket and places it on the shelf next to him. As he lights a cigarette he hears a noise. Nothing. He turns away, but as he is about to take a drag on his cigarette he hears something move.*

INT. ABANDONED HOUSE. NIGHT.

MATTHEW *wanders through the house toward where he heard the noise. He sees* MARIA *huddled in a corner. They stare at each other, then* MATTHEW *starts to move away.*

MARIA: What do you want?

MATTHEW: I don't want anything.

MARIA: Really.

MATTHEW: Yeah.

MARIA: Why?

MATTHEW: Because I don't think anything's going to help.

MARIA: What do you mean by that?

MATTHEW: You drink all that beer by yourself?

MARIA: Do you live around here?

MATTHEW: Not far.

MARIA: I don't have anywhere to go.

MATTHEW: So?

MARIA: Forget it.

    (MATTHEW *stands there, staring.*)

    So, what do you want?

MATTHEW: I said, I don't want anything.

MARIA: So then, get lost.

MATTHEW: What do *you* want?

MARIA: I don't want anything from you. That's for sure.

MATTHEW: Really?

MARIA: Yeah. Really.

    (MATTHEW *nods his head thoughtfully, then moves over and crouches down next to* MARIA.)

114

MATTHEW: Say it.
> (*It takes a good long time, but finally she lets down her defenses and sighs wearily.*)

MARIA: I . . . I need some place to sleep.

INT. MATTHEW'S BEDROOM. MORNING.

Books are strewn across the room. MARIA *is asleep in Matthew's bed. She wakes up and looks around her.*

EXT. MATTHEW'S HOUSE. MORNING.

MATTHEW *has been shopping. He comes up to the door, gets rid of his cigarette, and enters the house.*

INT. MATTHEW'S BEDROOM. MORNING.

MARIA *is sitting on the bed, reading a passage from Matthew's copy of* Man in the Universe. *It strikes her as strange, but intriguing. She puts the book down, but keeps looking at it, frowning.*

MATTHEW *enters with a small bag of groceries. He places before* MARIA *a bag of potato chips, a Coke, and a bottle of stomach medicine.*

MARIA: (*Of the medicine*) What are these?

MATTHEW: They'll make your stomach feel better.
> (MARIA *takes a sip of Coke.*)
> Where are you from?

MARIA: Around.

MATTHEW: Are you a runaway or something?

MARIA: I'm a murderer.

MATTHEW: (*Unfazed*) Really? Who'd you kill?

MARIA: Well, I'm not actually a murderer. But I've thought about killing myself.

MATTHEW: I know what you mean.

MARIA: You do?
> (MATTHEW *shows* MARIA *his grenade.*)

MATTHEW: I carry this with me at all times.

115

MARIA: A hand grenade?

MATTHEW: Yeah.

MARIA: Is it real?

MATTHEW: My dad brought it back from Korea.

MARIA: What for?

MATTHEW: Souvenir, I guess.

MARIA: No, I mean, why do you carry it around with you all the time?

MATTHEW: Just in case.

MARIA: Just in case what?

MATTHEW: Just in case.

MARIA: Are you emotionally disturbed?

MATTHEW: Look, I just showed it to you because of what you said.

MARIA: Forget what I said. Put that thing away.

MATTHEW: Do you really think it's a good idea to drink soda for breakfast?

MARIA: It keeps my skin clear.

MATTHEW: What?

MARIA: It's true.

MATTHEW: In ten years your bones are gonna snap like twigs. You oughta have a glass of milk.

MARIA: Milk gives me pimples.

MATTHEW: You probably get more pimples from all that makeup you're wearing.

MARIA: Makeup *hides* my pimples.

MATTHEW: Sorry.

MARIA: Do you live here alone?

MATTHEW: With my dad.

(MARIA *looks around nervously.*)

MARIA: Where is he?

MATTHEW: Visiting his sister. (*Pause.*) Well, I've got to go see this jerk about a job.

MARIA: Can I take a shower?

MATTHEW: Sure.

MARIA: Thanks.

(MATTHEW *looks at her.*)

MATTHEW: It's OK.

(MATTHEW *goes out.* MARIA *sits there a moment and realizes that her clothes stink.*)

116

INT. TV REPAIR OUTLET. DAY — A LITTLE LATER

There is a line of PEOPLE *holding broken TV sets that goes out the door and around the corner.* MATTHEW *enters. There is a guy about his age,* BRUCE, *working the front counter.* ANTHONY *is at the counter.*

ANTHONY: So, what's wrong with it?

BRUCE: Listen, cookie-puss, your warranty's expired. So just shut up and blow.

    (MATTHEW *shoves* ANTHONY *out of the way.*)

    What do you want?

MATTHEW: I'm here to see Mr. Santiago.

BRUCE: He ain't in.

MATTHEW: Get him.

BRUCE: What do you want?

SANTIAGO: (*Off*) Who is it, Bruce?

BRUCE: Nothing. Nothing much at all.

    (SANTIAGO *comes out.*)

SANTIAGO: So, Matthew.

    (MATTHEW *keeps his eyes lowered.*)

    Your father tells me you need a job.

MATTHEW: He tells me you need help.

SANTIAGO: Don't start in with me, Matthew! I'm only doing this for your father!

MATTHEW: I don't do TVs.

SANTIAGO: But TVs is what we fix.

MATTHEW: Television is the opium of the masses.

SANTIAGO: Matthew, be reasonable. I know you need a job. You know you need a job. It may not be what you're used to, but a paycheck's a paycheck.

MATTHEW: Radios. I'll fix radios. Phone answering machines. Calculators.

SANTIAGO: I don't need help with that stuff! Look, three hundred a week. I'll give you all the radios and appliances you want, *but* you've gotta work on TVs.

MATTHEW: Two hundred a week and I do only radios and appliances.

SANTIAGO: But I need *help* with the *TVs!*

MATTHEW: I'm sorry, I can't do it!

SANTIAGO: Jesus Christ! I'm just trying to do your old man a favor!

MATTHEW: I'm sure he appreciates it.

(MATTHEW *turns to leave, but first punches* BRUCE *in the stomach.*)

EXT. TV REPAIR OUTLET. DAY – MOMENTS LATER.

Customers fall back in fear as . . .
MATTHEW *throws open the door and steps out onto the sidewalk. He bumps into a* BLACK NURSE *and her TV falls to the sidewalk and is smashed. She and* MATTHEW *look down at it.*
MATTHEW: It was busted anyway. (*He stalks on.*)

INT. KITCHEN. DAY – MEANWHILE.

There is a washing machine and dryer in the large kitchen.
MARIA, *wrapped only in a big bath towel, throws her clothes in the machine, adds detergent, and turns it on. It rumbles into action. She lights a cigarette.*
She spots a toaster, finds some bread, and drops in a few slices. Picking up a glass of milk and a container with some cold soup, she goes over to the sink. She drops her cigarette into an old coffee cup, picks up a pan, and pours the soup into it. Noticing a radio, she reaches for it and turns it on – loud rock and roll music comes on. As she reaches for her glass of milk she knocks the pan of soup onto the floor. She looks at the mess, then picking up the glass of milk, she goes across the room, leaving the milk on the top of the washing machine where it trembles precariously.
MARIA *grabs hold of a sponge mop that is leaning against the wall, but her attention is diverted by . . .*
The newspaper headline . . .

INFANT KIDNAPPED AT BUS STOP

MARIA *picks the newspaper up. Preoccupied, she drops the paper, smells her hair, and goes out of the kitchen leaving behind her: the glass of milk trembling precariously on the edge of the washer, the cigarette floating in the dregs of the coffee cup, the soup on the floor, the bread burning in the toaster.*

INT. MATTHEW'S BATHROOM. DAY.

MARIA *washes her hair in the shower.*

EXT. MATTHEW'S FRONT YARD/DRIVEWAY. DAY – SAME TIME.

DAD *pulls up and steps out of his car.*

INT. MATTHEW'S KITCHEN. DAY – SAME TIME.

The radio is blaring . . . the toaster is on fire . . . the glass of milk is moving closer to the edge of the washing machine.

EXT. MATTHEW'S DRIVEWAY. DAY – SAME TIME.

DAD *closes the garage door.*

INT. MATTHEW'S KITCHEN. DAY – SAME TIME

The glass of milk topples over the edge of the washer and crashes onto the floor.

INT. MATTHEW'S BATHROOM. DAY – SAME TIME.

Pensive, MARIA *sits on the toilet seat smoking a cigarette.*

EXT. MATTHEW'S HOUSE. DAY – SAME TIME.

DAD *puts his key in the lock and enters the house.*

INT. MATTHEW'S BATHROOM. DAY – SAME TIME.

MARIA *gets up and puts the cigarette butt in the toilet as she leaves.*

INT. MATTHEW'S KITCHEN. DAY — SAME TIME.

DAD *surveys the damage.* MARIA *enters still wrapped in the bath towel.*

MARIA: Hi.

DAD: Who the hell are you?

MARIA: I'm a friend of your son's.

DAD: My son doesn't have any friends.

> (*At this point* MATTHEW *enters, sizes up the situation, and goes rigid with fear.* MARIA *and* DAD *look at him, waiting, but he just stares at the floor.* DAD *looks back at* MARIA, *fuming, then approaches* MATTHEW *and slaps him across the face.* MARIA *cringes.*)

What the hell is going on around here?

> (MATTHEW *is unable to speak. He opens his mouth, but can't form words. He is traumatized.* DAD *hits him again.* MARIA *steps forward.*)

Answer me!

MARIA: Hey!

DAD: (*To* MARIA) You keep outta this!

> (*To* MATTHEW.)

Answer me! Matthew!

MARIA: Why don't you just leave him alone!

DAD: Listen, missy, you better just put your clothes back on and get the hell outta my house!

MARIA: I'm going to put my clothes in that dryer and I'm going to wait until they are dry. And *then* I'll leave.

DAD: Is that right?

MARIA: Yeah, that's right.

DAD: Well, I've got news for you, you little harlot!

> (DAD *rushes over, throws open the machine, and drags Maria's clothes out, tossing them on the floor amongst the spilled milk and soup.*)

MARIA: (*To* MATTHEW) Are you all right?

> (MATTHEW *runs out the back door.*)

DAD: Matthew! Where are you going? Matthew! Get back here!

> (*To* MARIA.)

You better be gone when I get back.

> (DAD *runs out after* MATTHEW. MARIA *looks around at the*

*devastated kitchen. She bends down and lifts her soiled
clothes. She looks at them, sighs, and drops them to the
floor.)*

INT. MASTER BEDROOM. DAY—MOMENTS LATER.

MARIA *is poking around trying to find some clothes. She goes
toward the closet, opens it, and sees, naturally, only men's clothes.
But all the way in the back, she spots . . .
Some real old dresses. She reaches in and takes one out and then
leaves the room.*

INT. MATTHEW'S BEDROOM. DAY—MOMENTS LATER.

*With no makeup, her hair pulled back, and wearing the simple
dress,* MARIA *looks like a completely different person. She looks
down on the bed and sees the book,* Man and the Universe.

EXT. STREET. DAY.

MATTHEW *walking.*

EXT. STREETS. DAY THROUGH EVENING.

MARIA *spends the day walking around town, searching for*
MATTHEW. *There's no sign of him anywhere. She forges ahead as
evening falls . . .*

INT. BAR. NIGHT.

MATTHEW *is stooping to pick up some cigarettes from a machine.
He glares at* BRUCE *as he enters the bar.* PEG *notices his entrance.*
MATTHEW *looks particularly lethal this evening. The* DELI MAN
is watching TV and laughing. He has a patch over his eye.
MATTHEW *spins him around, punches him in the stomach, and
then pushes* ANTHONY *away from the bar.
The bartender,* PHIL, *approaches and turns off the TV, worried.*

PHIL: (*Panicked*) Matthew, really, sorry. Look, I'm turning it off!

(MATTHEW *takes a cassette tape from his pocket and thrusts it at* PHIL.)

MATTHEW: Play it and shut up. Bring me a bottle of scotch.

(*To someone on his left.*)

What the hell are you looking at?

(*Everyone in the place looks away and pretends to be calm.* PHIL *nervously shoves the cassette tape in the tape deck and comes back with a bottle of scotch as Beethoven starts filtering in over the sound system.*)

PHIL: Here you go, Matthew. On the house.

MATTHEW: Shut up.

(MATTHEW *grabs the bottle and steps further down the bar and pours himself a drink.*

PEG *sits herself down next to* MATTHEW.)

PEG: (*Of bottle*) How'd you know what I was drinking?

MATTHEW: (*Growls*) Get lost.

PEG: Your friend the bartender warned me about you.

MATTHEW: I don't have any friends.

PEG: He says women aren't very safe in here.

MATTHEW: Is that so?

PEG: I know some people who think you oughta be locked up.

MATTHEW: You gonna drink or you gonna talk?

(PEG *just looks at him, unintimidated. She's as tough as he is.*)

PEG: Oh, you really *are* fucked up.

MATTHEW: And you're not?

PEG: Well, at least I'm a grown-up.

MATTHEW: Listen, I don't wanna discuss your problems.

PEG: Then let's discuss yours.

MATTHEW: Why are you dressed in black?

PEG: Is that a *problem* for you?

MATTHEW: No, I just think a woman who comes into a bar like this, all dressed in black, may not be the kind of woman who likes to *talk* much.

PEG: Oh, but I love to talk.

MATTHEW: (*Sighs*) OK, what do you want to talk about?

PEG: (*Coy*) Oh, I don't know. Nothing in particular. The weather, maybe.

MATTHEW: The weather sucks.

PEG: I think it's kinda warm for this time of year, don't you think?

MATTHEW: It's the damage to the ozone.

PEG: What?

MATTHEW: Ozone.

PEG: What's that?

MATTHEW: It keeps the sun's ultraviolet rays from burning us up! Where the hell you been the last ten years?

PEG: Married.

MATTHEW: I don't think this conversation's going anywhere.

PEG: Sure it is. I'm learning all this stuff about the ozone.

MATTHEW: Great.

PEG: So, do you have a girlfriend?

MATTHEW: What's *that* got to do with anything?

PEG: Maybe that's your problem.

MATTHEW: Do I have a problem?

PEG: Of course you do.

MATTHEW: Oh yeah, and what do *you* think my problem is?

PEG: I don't think you get laid enough.

MATTHEW: Is that so?

PEG: Well, what kind of relationship could a man as screwed up as you possibly have?

MATTHEW: I don't have relationships.

PEG: You love 'em and leave 'em, huh?

MATTHEW: I don't *love* anybody.

PEG: You mean, you just *have* a girl.

MATTHEW: I take what I can get. Now if you're through talking, do you want to go out back and fuck?

PEG: (*Speechless*) You're talking to the mother of two. You know that! You can't be talking to somebody's mother like that. Bastard!

(MATTHEW *gives her a glass.*)

MATTHEW: Here, have a drink.

PEG: Oh, fuck off.

MATTHEW: No, seriously. I mean it. Stay. (*He pours her a drink.*)

PEG: Everything's been very screwed up since my divorce. He took the kids away from me like I'm unfit or something.

MATTHEW: Have you got a car?

(MARIA *enters and comes toward* MATTHEW, *exhausted. She doesn't notice* PEG.)

MARIA: (*To* MATTHEW) *There* you are! I've been looking all over for you!

PEG: Maria!

MARIA: (*Surprised*) Peg!

MATTHEW: Where'd you get that dress?

PEG: (*To* MARIA) Do you *know* him?

MARIA: (*To* MATTHEW) Matthew, come home with us.

PEG: What!

MARIA: (*To* PEG) He has to, Peg.

PEG: Maria, if you go home now, Mom's gonna stab you in the heart with a steak knife, OK?

MATTHEW: (*Realizing*) You two are sisters?

MARIA: Don't go back to your father's house.

MATTHEW: I have to go back.

MARIA: Why?

MATTHEW: I have to.

MARIA: Matthew, he's a monster.

PEG: What's going on here?

MARIA: (*To* PEG) Matthew's coming home to live with us for a while.

PEG: (*Outraged*) Maria, do you *know* who this guy is?

MARIA: I don't care who he is.

(*Then, to* MATTHEW.)

Who are you?

PEG: Maybe he doesn't want to come home with us!

(*The girls look at* MATTHEW. *He looks away.*)

MATTHEW: Leave me alone.

PEG: (*Relieved*) There, OK? Come on Maria. Let's get outta here.

(PEG *gets up.* MARIA *stays there and stares into Matthew's face as he gazes at his hands on the bar before him. A few moments pass, then . . .*)

MARIA: Are you sure?

MATTHEW: (*Lies*) Yeah.

PEG: Maria, come on!

(MARIA *stares at him a moment longer.*)

MARIA: (*To* MATTHEW) Please come back to the house with me.
MATTHEW: (*Looks at her*) Why?
MARIA: (*Honestly*) I'm afraid of my mother.

INT. MARIA'S KITCHEN. NIGHT.

JEAN *is sitting alone at the kitchen table, dressed in black, drinking gin and staring at the floor. She notices a roast chicken by the sink and picks up the carving knife to cut it when the back door opens.*
MARIA, PEG, *and* MATTHEW *clamber in the back door and crowd into a little frightened huddle when they see . . .*
JEAN *with the knife in her hand.*
MARIA *slowly pushes her way past the others and comes forward into the kitchen.*
JEAN *stands still, not looking at the others.*
PEG *and* MATTHEW *watch from the doorway.* PEG *is nervous.*
MATTHEW *is confused.*
MARIA *moves toward* JEAN, *who turns around pointing the knife at her.*

PEG: (*Leaving the room*) Christ!
  (MARIA *and* JEAN *stare each other down for a moment,*
  then . . .)
JEAN: (*Ice*) I'm never gonna forgive you.
MARIA: I know.
JEAN: As long as I live I'm gonna work your fingers to the
  bone.
MARIA: OK.
JEAN: Did you eat anything today?
MARIA: (*Weak*) No.
JEAN: (*Turns away*) Sit down. I'll fix you something.
  (*Looks back at* MATTHEW.)
  Who's your friend?

INT. MARIA'S KITCHEN. NIGHT.

They're all sitting or standing around the kitchen. JEAN *brushes*
Maria's hair.
MARIA: . . . so then he gives me *back* the five dollars and still
  wants me to kiss him.
PEG: Oh, gross!
JEAN: Disgusting . . .
MARIA: I was so scared. And he's like sweating and rubbing
  his crotch and everything . . .
PEG: So, what'd you do?
MARIA: What'd you think I did?
MATTHEW: You burned him with the cigarette.
MARIA: Right in the eye.
PEG: Ouch!
JEAN: That man is going straight to hell.
MARIA: And he's threatening to call the cops on *me*.
MATTHEW: So, was this before or after the baby disappeared?
MARIA: Just before it.
PEG: You've gotta go to the police, Maria.
JEAN: Yes, that man should be punished!
PEG: No, about the baby.
MARIA: Well, I don't know. I can't be sure. I didn't *see* anything.
PEG: But at least they could talk to her.
MARIA: She seemed so sad. So mixed up.

PEG: We're all mixed up, Maria, but we don't go around stealing babies.

MARIA: You see, you're already convinced that she did it.

PEG: (*To* MARIA) So, what are you gonna do?

MARIA: About what?

PEG: About being pregnant.

JEAN: (*To* MATTHEW) You ain't the father, are you?

MATTHEW: No, ma'am.

MARIA: (*Embarrassed*) Mom!

JEAN: (*To* MARIA) Eat your sandwich!

MARIA: (*To* PEG) I went to the clinic yesterday and I spoke to this lady . . .

PEG: How much?

MARIA: I'd need about two hundred and fifty dollars.
(*She looks at* JEAN.)

JEAN: What, for an abortion? Don't look at me. I spent everything we had on your father's casket.
(MARIA *looks to* PEG, *who shrugs sadly.*)

PEG: The divorce lawyers took all my money.
(MARIA *shrugs and accepts the burden.*)

MARIA: Then I'll get a job.

MATTHEW: I've got money.

MARIA: No, thank you.

MATTHEW: It's OK.

PEG: Why don't you get it from Anthony?

MARIA: I don't ever want to see that jerk again.

MATTHEW: Take the money from me.

MARIA: No. You don't have a job either.

MATTHEW: I'm going to take this job fixing TVs.

PEG: Maria, where'd you get that dress?
(MARIA *looks at* MATTHEW *and bites her lip.* PEG *and* JEAN *follow her gaze to* . . .
MATTHEW *as he calmly regards the dress* . . .)

MATTHEW: It belonged to my mother.

INT. MARIA'S UPSTAIRS HALLWAY. NIGHT.

From the hall, we see MARIA *dismantling her room. It is a typically tasteless teenage girl's room. She's tearing posters off the*

127

walls. Then she lugs a mattress through the hall and into the next room. PEG *comes up the stairs and goes into her own room.*

INT. PEG'S BEDROOM. NIGHT.

MATTHEW *is fixing Peg's TV. He sets it upright, turns it on, and it works.*
PEG: You fix it?
MATTHEW: Yeah.
PEG: Thanks.
MATTHEW: You're welcome.
PEG: You wanna watch some TV?
MATTHEW: I don't watch TV.
PEG: Why not?
MATTHEW: It gives you cancer.
PEG: It does not.
MATTHEW: (*Shrugs*) Well, see for yourself.
    (MARIA *appears in the hall beside* MATTHEW *with the book she took from his room.*)
MARIA: Do you know what the word "empirical" means?
PEG: Don't ask him. He thinks TV gives you cancer.
MATTHEW: It means information based on experience.
    (MARIA *shakes her head in confusion.*)
    You can't know something unless you experience it first.
    (PEG *rolls her eyes in exasperation and closes her door.*)
PEG: Jesus!
    (MARIA *and* MATTHEW *are alone in the hall a moment. He sees the book she is holding.*)
MARIA: I borrowed it. Do you mind?
MATTHEW: No.
MARIA: I put a bed in here for you.
    (*They look in at the bed.*)
MATTHEW: Where do you sleep?
MARIA: (*Of her room*) I sleep in there.
MATTHEW: (*Looks in*) There's no bed in here.
MARIA: I don't need one.
MATTHEW: Are you nearsighted?
MARIA: Yeah.
MATTHEW: Why don't you wear your glasses?

MARIA: They make me look stupid.

MATTHEW: How do you mean?

MARIA: You know, brainy, like a librarian.

MATTHEW: I like librarians.

> (MARIA *waits a moment, then puts on her glasses and lets him see.*
>
> MATTHEW *is immobilized by desire* — MARIA *sees this, blushing.*
>
> MARIA *waits expectantly, watching as he leans toward her* — *seemingly against his will.*
>
> MARIA *lifts her face to be kissed, breathless and still. Matthew's face comes toward hers. They both linger* — *unsure. A moment.*
>
> *Then* MATTHEW *moves back.*
>
> MARIA *stands there, dizzy, looking at the floor.*
>
> MATTHEW *stands back, also looking at the floor.*)

MARIA: (*Weakly*) Give me your hand grenade.

MATTHEW: (*Looks up*) What?

MARIA: Give it to me.

> (MARIA *puts out her hand.*
>
> MATTHEW *reaches into his pocket and takes it out. He hands it over.*
>
> JEAN *appears at the bottom of the stairs.*)

JEAN: Maria!

> (MARIA *jumps into her room and closes the door.*
>
> MATTHEW *remains in the hallway looking down at* JEAN, *who is still at the bottom of the stairs.*)

I don't want you getting any ideas.

MATTHEW: Ideas about what?

JEAN: You know what. Tomorrow you find somewhere else to sleep. Get it?

MATTHEW: OK.

JEAN: I don't know what your problem is, but I've got problems of my own!

> (MATTHEW *nods as* JEAN *moves away. He then goes toward his own room.*)

INT. MARIA'S ROOM. NIGHT.

MARIA *looks at the grenade in her hand and then puts it in the top drawer of her desk. She then closes the drawer, picks up her pen, and starts writing in her notebook . . .*

MARIA: (*Writing*) I am ashamed. I am ashamed of being young. I am ashamed of being stupid.
(MARIA *pauses, closes her notebook, and turns off the light. She curls up on the floor, pulling a blanket over her. She takes off her glasses and closes her eyes.*)

INT. MARIA'S KITCHEN. DAY.

MARIA *is doing the laundry, while* PEG *sits at the table with her friend* LORI, *who is about Peg's age (twenty-eight).*
From now on, MARIA *only wears the dress she took from Matthew's house. She usually wears her glasses and her hair is pulled back away from her face.*

LORI: (*To* MARIA) So, have you been over to the clinic?
MARIA: Yes.
LORI: Are you gonna have an abortion?
MARIA: I suppose.
PEG: I think that's the right move.
MARIA: (*To* PEG) Did you ever have one?
PEG: An abortion?
MARIA: Yeah.
PEG: Sure.
LORI: When?
PEG: A couple of years ago.
MARIA: After you'd already had children?
PEG: Exactly.
MARIA: Why?
PEG: Well, because I already had two kids I couldn't handle. And I hated my husband.
LORI: My second baby saved my marriage.
PEG: My marriage was beyond saving.
MARIA: (*To* LORI) Did you have the baby *because* your marriage needed help?

130

LORI: Definitely. But then, I really did want another baby. I like being pregnant.

MARIA: (*To* PEG) Did you want to get pregnant the first time?

PEG: I suppose. We didn't think about it. When we first got married we just spent all our time fucking. I mean, what the hell; we were married, right? Pretty soon I got pregnant and that was OK 'cause I was already kinda bored with my husband. I was seventeen.

MARIA: (*To* LORI) How old were you when you got married?

LORI: Twenty.

MARIA: Did you want to have children right away?

LORI: Oh, yeah. I couldn't wait.

MARIA: Do you ever think about what your life might've been like if you never got married and had kids?

LORI: (*Thinks, then* . . .) No.

MARIA: Never?

LORI: Well, what's the use in thinking about *that* now?

MARIA: Did you think about it then?

LORI: Of course not. Did you, Peg?

PEG: (*Shakes her head "no"*) Who thinks about that stuff when you're seventeen years old?

(PEG *and* LORI *turn silently and look at* MARIA.)

INT. FACTORY. DAY.

An older WOMAN *is showing* MARIA *how to do assembly line work. They are standing in front of a big drill press–type machine.*

WOMAN: Now, you just stand here, like this, and take one of these slugs and you put it right in here where the groove is. Then, you press down on the pedal down here, see, with your foot. Like this. You pull down on this arm here till the drill goes right through to the mark, here. You got that?

MARIA: Right.

WOMAN: Then you let go of the arm and take your foot off the pedal. Let go of the arm *first*. Remember that.

MARIA: Let go of the arm first.

WOMAN: Right. You gotta let go of the arm first or you damage the whole machine.

MARIA: OK.

WOMAN: So, when you take your foot off the pedal, you just knock the slug off the plate and toss it into this barrel over here . . .

(*The* WOMAN *proceeds to demonstrate the process.*)

INT. FACTORY. DAY – LATER.

MARIA, *wearing goggles and a smock, works at the machine.*

INT. TV REPAIR OUTLET. DAY.

MATTHEW *works on TVs.*

EXT. TRAIN STATION. LATE AFTERNOON.

MARIA *comes across the street and meets* MATTHEW, *who is sitting at the base of a column.*

MARIA: Hi.

MATTHEW: How was work?

MARIA: Do you know how to type?

MATTHEW: I'm not good at it.

MARIA: I've got to learn how to type. Typing has to be better than drilling holes in little pieces of aluminum all day. (*Pause.*) What time is it?

MATTHEW: Five to five.

EXT. TRAIN PLATFORM. AFTERNOON – MOMENTS LATER.

MARIA *and* MATTHEW *stand at the bottom of the stairs leading up to the train platform.*

MATTHEW: Who are we waiting for?

MARIA: The husband of the lady I met on the bench.

MATTHEW: How do you know what he looks like?

MARIA: I remember her saying he carried a briefcase and smokes a pipe.

MATTHEW: A lot of men fit that description.

MARIA: Yeah, but I think we'll know this guy when we see him.

MATTHEW: Why?

MARIA: He'll seem childish. Like a boy. Kinda nave.

> (*They watch the stairs. Then* MATTHEW *frowns to himself and looks at* MARIA.)

MATTHEW: Kind of what?

MARIA: Nave.

MATTHEW: Nave?

> (MARIA *looks at* MATTHEW *and becomes uncertain. She takes out a small notebook she carries with her and flips the pages until . . .*
> *She points out a word.*)
> "Naive."

MARIA: Naive?

MATTHEW: Naive.

MARIA: Oh.

> (*Up above they hear . . .*
> *The train pull into the station.*
> MATTHEW *and* MARIA *move closer to the stairs.*
> *The train slowly screeches to a halt.*
> *They wait anxiously, their eyes peeled on . . .*
> *The top of the stairs.*
> *The train doors open and a mass of feet shuffle out toward the stairs and . . .*
> *Down the steps and stop, suddenly as one.*
> MATTHEW *and* MARIA *stand there, blocking the bottom of the stairs, staring curiously up at . . .*
> *The dozens of* MEN *standing on the stairs, all dressed exactly alike, holding briefcases and with pipes in their mouths. The* MEN *look down just as curiously at . . .*
> MATTHEW *and* MARIA. MARIA *looks at* MATTHEW, *shrugs her shoulders, and walks away.*)

INT. MARIA'S KITCHEN. EVENING.

MATTHEW *is repairing an old electric typewriter at the kitchen table. The girls are finishing their meal.* JEAN *pours herself a gin and glances at* MATTHEW.

JEAN: (*To* MATTHEW) Still here, huh?

MARIA: Mom, he has nowhere to go.

JEAN: Shut up, you, and finish those potatoes!

MARIA: Mom, if I eat anything else I'll explode.

JEAN: Eat 'em! And when you're through get started on those dishes!

MATTHEW: This is a well built piece of machinery.

JEAN: They don't make things like they used to.

PEG: Mom, you never told us you were a secretary.

JEAN: I hated it. I hated working. I was so glad when your father proposed.

PEG: Don't you consider being a wife and mother work?

JEAN: With the likes of you two it was torture.

MARIA: Do you ever think of going back out to work?

JEAN: Never! *You're* going to support me! For the rest of my life you'll have to make sure there's food in my mouth and clothes on my back! Got it? Now, eat those potatoes!

MARIA: OK! OK!

JEAN: It's not gonna be easy!

MARIA: I know!

JEAN: You'll have to work every minute of your life!

PEG: Mom, ease up. Maybe you oughta lie down.

JEAN: Peg, don't play up to me.

(MATTHEW *flips a switch and the typewriter activates.*)

MATTHEW: OK. That's it.

(MATTHEW *turns to* MARIA *and pushes the typewriter over to her.*)

JEAN: I never wanted daughters in the first place.

(MARIA *puts on her glasses and begins to operate the machine.*)

You'll have to type faster than that to keep us out of the poorhouse.

(MARIA *looks off into space.*)

INT. MARIA'S KITCHEN. NIGHT – LATER.

MARIA *has finished mopping the floor and is putting the mop and bucket away. She moves through the living room, passing* JEAN *on the sofa.*

MARIA: Goodnight, Mom.
(JEAN *glances up at* MARIA, *pensively.*)

INT. PEG'S BEDROOM. NIGHT.

PEG *is lying on the bed in her bathrobe, watching TV.* MARIA
enters and lies on the bed next to her.
MARIA: Do you miss your kids?
PEG: Sure.
MARIA: Do you hate your husband?
PEG: Absolutely.
MARIA: Would you ever get married again?
PEG: Of course.

INT. MARIA'S KITCHEN. NIGHT—SAME TIME.

JEAN *enters the dark kitchen and finds* MATTHEW *sitting at the
table smoking and drinking scotch.* JEAN *sits down opposite him.*
JEAN: Why aren't you asleep?
MATTHEW: I don't sleep.
JEAN: Aren't you a little old to be running around with a
    seventeen-year-old?
MATTHEW: You want me to go?
JEAN: (*Shrugs*) I don't know.
MATTHEW: I'm not here to cause trouble.
JEAN: There's no avoiding trouble.
MATTHEW: (*Carefully*) You ride Maria pretty hard.
JEAN: How I raise my kids is none of your business.
MATTHEW: (*Looks away*) Sorry.
JEAN: You like *her* more than Peg, don't you?
MATTHEW: Who said anything about Peg?
JEAN: I think Peg's prettier.
MATTHEW: They're both pretty.
JEAN: Peg's more levelheaded too, but she's wild. Always been
    like that. Made a mess of her marriage.
MATTHEW: Maria sleeps on the floor.
JEAN: You really do like her more, huh.
MATTHEW: I don't like to see her torture herself.
JEAN: Have you two been screwing around?

136

(*The two of them stare at each other. They hold it for a moment. Then* MATTHEW *breaks it and reaches for his cigarette pack and offers* JEAN *one.*)

MATTHEW: Want a cigarette?

JEAN: Don't change the subject.

MATTHEW: I haven't touched her.

JEAN: (*Taking the cigarette*) I don't think she knows much about how to make love to a man.

MATTHEW: She must know something. She's pregnant.

JEAN: That's what I mean. A girl who knows how to make love to a man would never let that happen.

MATTHEW: You think so?

JEAN: You stand a better chance with Peg, you know. And I bet she's great in bed.

(JEAN *leans forward so that* MATTHEW *can light her cigarette.*)

MATTHEW: (*Pauses, then lights her cigarette*) We don't have much in common.

JEAN: When was the last time you were with a woman?

MATTHEW: I don't remember.

JEAN: (*Turns away from* MATTHEW) I'm never going to let you take Maria away from me.

MATTHEW: I never said I wanted to.

JEAN: She's got to pay.

MATTHEW: Your husband died of a heart attack.

JEAN: No one dies of a heart attack. They die of disgust, disappointment.

MATTHEW: You're not the first woman in the world who's had a hard time.

JEAN: You're an outsider; you don't understand. A family's got to stick together, come hell or high water.

MATTHEW: A family's like a gun. You point it in the wrong direction, you're gonna kill somebody.

JEAN: Exactly.

(MATTHEW *looks at* JEAN.)

INT. MATTHEW'S BEDROOM. NIGHT.

MARIA *is sitting on Matthew's bed holding the hand grenade.*
MATTHEW *enters.*

MATTHEW: You've gotta leave this house.

MARIA: I have to take care of my mother.

MATTHEW: Your mother is a psychopath.

MARIA: She's just in pain.

MATTHEW: (*Pause*) What are you doing here?

MARIA: How does this work?

MATTHEW: What do you want to know that for? Give me that thing. (*He goes toward the bed.*)

MARIA: No, how's it work?

MATTHEW: Why?

MARIA: I just want to know.

(MATTHEW *sits down close to* MARIA *on the bed.*)

MATTHEW: (*Points*) You see this pin? You pull that, wait eight seconds, and then . . .

MARIA: . . . boom.

MATTHEW: (*Touching her*) Sleep in here tonight. (*Moves his hand away.*) I don't mean with me. I just mean, sleep here. In a bed.

MARIA: Peg says you have a reputation.

MATTHEW: What kind of reputation?

MARIA: A dangerous reputation.

MATTHEW: Peg's got a reputation herself.

MARIA: I wanna become a nun.

MATTHEW: No you don't.

MARIA: Yes I do.

MATTHEW: No you *don't*. You're just having some kind of severe reaction.

MARIA: I don't want to feel anything.

MATTHEW: Well, I bet nuns feel things. You have to be dead not to feel things. You don't want to be dead, do you? (MARIA *turns toward* MATTHEW. *They look at each other and then kiss, tenderly. They stay with their foreheads touching, and then* MARIA *turns her head toward the grenade in her hand and* MATTHEW *looks away.*)

MARIA: I'm gonna go to the clinic tomorrow to have the abortion. Will you come with me?

MATTHEW: If you want me to.

MARIA: Why do you do this?

MATTHEW: Do what?

MARIA: Why do you hang around here and look after me like this?

MATTHEW: Somebody has to.

MARIA: Why you?

INT. CLINIC. DAY.

MARIA *and* MATTHEW *are sitting on chairs in the waiting room.*
MATTHEW *puts a cigarette in his mouth. They both look anxious.*
MATTHEW: How long do you think it'll take?

MARIA: I don't know. Not long, I guess.

MATTHEW: Are you OK?

MARIA: Yeah. You? (*She takes the cigarette out of Matthew's mouth.*)

MATTHEW: I feel like smashing things up.

MARIA: Relax. There's nothing to worry about. Why don't you go for a walk?

MATTHEW: I don't want to take a walk. You sure you want to go through with this?

MARIA: What do you mean?

MATTHEW: Marry me.

MARIA: Don't be crazy.

MATTHEW: Marry me. Have the baby. We'll be a family.

MARIA: You're delirious.

MATTHEW: Sorry.

MARIA: It's OK.

(MATTHEW *breathes nervously.*)

MATTHEW: How long do you think it'll take?

MARIA: I don't know. Not long, I guess.

(*She takes the cigarette out of Matthew's mouth.*)

MATTHEW: Are you OK?

MARIA: Yeah. You?

MATTHEW: I feel like tearing somebody's head off.

VOICE: (*Off*) Maria Coughlin.

(MARIA *and* MATTHEW *look at each other, then* MARIA *resolutely gets up.*

MATTHEW *sighs, then looks at the other women in the room. He also glances at a guy,* JOHN, *sitting among the women.* JOHN *comes and sits down next to* MATTHEW.)

139

JOHN: How're you doin'?

MATTHEW: I feel like smashing things up.

JOHN: Yeah. Sometimes it gets like that. Your first time?

MATTHEW: What?

JOHN: Your first time here?

MATTHEW: Of course.

JOHN: I thought so.

MATTHEW: Who the hell are you?

JOHN: John. John Bill. How're you doin'?

(JOHN *puts his hand out for* MATTHEW *to shake.* MATTHEW *ignores it.*)

MATTHEW: I already told you. I feel like punchin' somebody's lights out.

JOHN: Yeah. The first time's kinda tough. But you know, it's an amazing thing. You come in here the first time—your whole life's a mess. All this tension and stuff. Then she goes in there and when she comes out everything's fixed.

(MATTHEW *looks at him, then he grabs* JOHN *and throws him to the floor. People scream as* MATTHEW *and* JOHN *grapple with each other on the floor.*

In the other room MARIA *is taking off her jacket. She stops when she hears the noise of fighting. She jumps off the table and goes out into the waiting room.*)

EXT. PARKING LOT NEAR TRAIN STATION. DAY — LATER.

MARIA *and* MATTHEW *are sitting by the column.*

MARIA: What time is it?

MATTHEW: Five-o-three.

MARIA: Did you mean it? Would you marry me?

MATTHEW: Yes.

MARIA: Why?

MATTHEW: Because I want to.

MARIA: Not because you love me or anything like that, huh?

MATTHEW: I respect and admire you.

MARIA: Isn't that love?

MATTHEW: No. That's respect and admiration. I think that's better than love.

MARIA: How?

MATTHEW: When people are in love they do all sorts of crazy things. They get jealous, they lie, they cheat. They kill themselves. They kill each other.

MARIA: It doesn't have to be that way.

MATTHEW: Maybe.

MARIA: You'd be the father of a child you know isn't yours.

MATTHEW: Kids are kids, what does it matter?

MARIA: Do you trust me?

MATTHEW: Do you trust me first?

MARIA: I trust you.

MATTHEW: You sure?

MARIA: Yes.

(MATTHEW *looks at* MARIA *and then kneels down in front of her.*)

MATTHEW: Then marry me.

MARIA: I'll marry you if you admit that respect, admiration, and trust equals love.

MATTHEW: OK. They equal love.

(MARIA *and* MATTHEW *kiss.* MARIA *looks at* MATTHEW, *then removing her glasses she climbs to the top of the base of the column and, turning around, falls backward off the base.* MATTHEW *runs and . . . catches her in his arms, shocked. She opens her eyes and smiles up at him.* MATTHEW *can't speak. He's gone white as a sheet.*)

MARIA: Good. I trust you. Now it's your turn. (*She rolls out of his arms and stands at the foot of the column base.*)

MATTHEW: What?

MARIA: Go on up.

MATTHEW: Maria, that's pretty high.

MARIA: Don't you trust me?

MATTHEW: Of course I do.

MARIA: Then go on up.

MATTHEW: Maria, I'm twice your size. If I fall on you from that height I'll kill you.

MARIA: Trust me.

(MATTHEW *hesitates. He looks at the column base and then back at her.*)

MATTHEW: This is not a matter of trust.

MARIA: Matthew, go up. I will break your fall. I promise.

141

(MATTHEW *holds her resolute gaze for a while, then sighs and heads up. He reaches the top and hesitates again.*)

MATTHEW: If I do this, will you leave your mother?

MARIA: What?

MATTHEW: You heard me.

MARIA: Maybe.

MATTHEW: Not good enough.

MARIA: You're being selfish.

MATTHEW: The woman's a sadist.

MARIA: She's just in shock. What's a sadist?

MATTHEW: Your mother or me.

MARIA: Wait a minute. Look!

(MARIA *walks over to the parking lot.* MATTHEW *follows.*)

EXT. PARKING LOT. DAY.

MARIA *is crouched in front of a car's bumper. There is a sticker on it advertising Cape Holiday.*

MATTHEW: What is it?

MARIA: The woman said she and her husband go to Cape
   Holiday every summer.

MATTHEW: (*Looking around the lot.*) There's another one.
(MARIA *follows his gaze and sees* . . .
A Cape Holiday sticker on another car.)
MARIA: (*Points*) And over there too. There might be dozens.
MATTHEW: But how many belong to *men* who take the five-fifteen *train*?

DISSOLVE TO . . .

EXT. STATION. DAY—MOMENTS LATER.

The five-fifteen pulls out of the station.
MARIA *and* MATTHEW *come walking up between an aisle of cars,
scrutinizing the bumpers.* MARIA *writes in her notebook* . . .
MARIA: (*Calculating*) Seven.
MATTHEW: And there were ten before the five-fifteen came
through.
MARIA: The white fancy one is gone.
MATTHEW: The yellow pickup truck. The Japanese model.
Three.
MARIA: Three.
MATTHEW: What are you going to do when you find this man?
MARIA: I don't know yet.

INT. MARIA'S LIVING ROOM. EVENING.

PEG *is sitting on the sofa watching TV.* JEAN *comes in and sits
beside her.*
JEAN: Peg, don't you think Matthew's a handsome man?
PEG: He's OK.
JEAN: Why haven't you made a play for him?
PEG: Mom!
JEAN: What?
PEG: You're unbelievable.
JEAN: He's too old for Maria.
PEG: So, what do you want me to do about it?
JEAN: Throw yourself at him.
PEG: Mom, I do not *throw* myself at men, OK?
JEAN: You used to.

143

PEG: Shut up and watch TV.

JEAN: Don't snap at me like that.

PEG: He's not interested in me.

JEAN: That's what you think.

PEG: What do you mean?

JEAN: I've seen the way he looks at you.

PEG: Yeah, right. And *I've* seen the way he looks at Maria.

JEAN: Oh, you're just imagining it. He likes you. I can tell.

PEG: You can?

JEAN: She isn't giving him *any*.

PEG: You're kidding me.

JEAN: God's honest truth.

PEG: Really.

JEAN: Think about it.

INT. RUARK COMPUTER FACTORY. DAY.

MATTHEW *is trying to get his job back. He is talking to the big* BOSS, *an attractive and aggressive young woman.*

BOSS: What can I do for you, Matthew?

MATTHEW: I'd like my job back.

BOSS: That's impossible.

MATTHEW: I'm sorry about vicing Ed's head.

BOSS: That's not what I'm talking about.

MATTHEW: What?

BOSS: You lied to us.

MATTHEW: When?

BOSS: When you applied for this job you said you had attended MIT.

MATTHEW: Did I say that?

BOSS: And you never told us about your police record and four years of reform school.

MATTHEW: You never asked.

BOSS: We gave you a lot of responsibility.

MATTHEW: I did a good job.

BOSS: That's beside the point.

MATTHEW: What difference does it make?

BOSS: I can't do it.

MATTHEW: Why not?

144

BOSS: People are afraid of you.

MATTHEW: I'll be nice. Really, I promise.

BOSS: Are you working now?

MATTHEW: Yes.

BOSS: For a competitor?

MATTHEW: I fix televisions.

BOSS: Well, work is work . . .

MATTHEW: I need something stable. With benefits. Pension plan–type stuff, you know.

BOSS: Why the sudden interest in stability?

MATTHEW: I'm getting married.

BOSS: Really?

MATTHEW: Listen, I promise I won't lose my temper anymore. I won't make a fuss about bad manufacturing or faulty designs. I won't *care* about *quality* at all. I just want a job with normal benefits for me and my dependents.
(*The* BOSS *looks away and considers.*
MATTHEW *waits.*)

BOSS: I can't give you your old job back.

MATTHEW: I'll take anything.

BOSS: Eligibility for benefits starts after six months.

MATTHEW: Fine.

BOSS: You'll have to take a few steps down.

INT. MATTHEW'S TV ROOM. DAY.

DAD *is watching TV. He looks sad. He looks at the TV, then stands up and with a determined look on his face, pulls the plug out.*
The TV tube goes dead.

INT. TV REPAIR OUTLET. DAY.

DAD *walks in carrying his TV.* BRUCE *is standing by a set of TV monitors.* DAD *sets his TV down in front of* BRUCE.

BRUCE: Can I help you?

DAD: (*Looking around*) My TV's busted.

BRUCE: Just leave it here. I'll have a look at it later on.

DAD: Where's Matthew?

BRUCE: He doesn't work here anymore.
DAD: What?
BRUCE: He got fired.
DAD: You mean he quit.
BRUCE: No, I mean he got fired.
DAD: Bullshit. Nobody in their right mind would fire
  Matthew. He can fix anything.
BRUCE: Look, I'm telling you. He got fired. He scared the
  customers.
DAD: Well, what the hell do the customers know? Matthew's a
  genius.
BRUCE: Well, we don't need a genius. We need somebody who
  can fix TVs.
DAD: Yeah. Well, that's your problem, pal. (*He leaves the shop.*)
BRUCE: What do you want me to do with this TV?
DAD: Get the damn thing out of my sight!

EXT. TV REPAIR OUTLET. DAY.

DAD *thinks for a moment, then walks away.*

INT. FACTORY. DAY.

MARIA *is operating her machine.*
MARIA: (*Voice over*) "Vicissitude: 1a, the quality or state of
  being changeable; mutability; b, natural change or
  mutation visible in human nature or human affairs; 2a, a
  favorable or unfavorable event or situation that occurs by
  chance . . ." (*She turns away from the machine and looks
  at the clock.*)

EXT. TRAIN STATION. DAY.

MARIA: (*Reading from her notebook*) "Fluctuation of state or
condition; alternating change. See change."
  (MARIA *looks up, hearing . . .*
  The five-fifteen pull into the station.
  She jumps up and runs to a position where she can see . . .

146

The yellow Plymouth . . .
The station wagon . . .
And the Japanese model.
COMMUTERS *come stampeding down the stairs.*
MARIA *looks over as . . .*
COMMUTERS *fan out into the parking lot.*
She looks back and forth between the cars.
She sees a MAN *with a pipe unlock one of the cars. As* MARIA
comes toward the car, he looks up and faints.
MARIA *crouches over his prone body.*
She shakes him.)
Mister.
(*The man,* ROBERT, *does not respond.* MARIA *turns toward
the briefcase lying beside him and pulls out the tag with his
name and address.* ROBERT *revives.*)

ROBERT: Who are you?
MARIA: My name's Maria.
ROBERT: What do you want?
MARIA: I think I know your wife.
   (ROBERT *just looks at her, stone-faced, then away. He sighs
   wearily and gets up off the ground.*
   *Reaching the driver's side door, he puts the key in the lock,
   and pauses. He thinks a moment.*
   MARIA *hovers behind him.*)
ROBERT: What do you intend to do?
MARIA: (*Careful*) I was in trouble and she gave me some
   money. I just want to return it.
   (MARIA *comes over to* ROBERT *with five dollars.*
   He just looks at it.
   She holds it closer.
   He takes it.)
   What's her name?
ROBERT: Who?
MARIA: Your wife's.
ROBERT: Rachel.
MARIA: Will you tell her I said thank you?
ROBERT: (*Hesitates*) Yes.
   (*Another moment of awkward silence, then* MARIA *walks*

away. ROBERT *hurries into his car, slamming the door behind him.*

MARIA *stands back as he pulls out and speeds away.*)

INT. RUARK COMPUTER FACTORY. DAY — MEANWHILE.

ED *is at his workbench.* MATTHEW *approaches him.*

MATTHEW: Ed.

ED: (*Defensively*) What is it?

MATTHEW: Calm down, Ed.

ED: What do you want?

MATTHEW: I just happened to notice that these circuit boards we're wiring into the new models are the A-67-9's.

ED: Brilliant. So what?

MATTHEW: We manufactured these boards last year and too high a percentage of them proved faulty in these higher powered, larger memory units so we stored them out back.

ED: I know that, Slaughter.

MATTHEW: Well, I just thought maybe there's been some kind of mistake or something.

ED: Why do you always have to be such a pain in the neck?

MATTHEW: I'm just doing my job.

ED: Your job is to put these things together the way we tell you to.

(MATTHEW *obviously wants to rip Ed's lungs out, but has to control himself.*)

MATTHEW: Right.

(ED *decides to be big about it and opens his specifications manual. He flips through the pages as* MATTHEW, *smiling, looks on over his shoulder.*)

ED: (*Points*) There. You see, part A-67-9. See it?

MATTHEW: (*Frowns*) Yeah, I see it.

ED: Satisfied?

(MATTHEW *doesn't answer.*)

INT. MARIA'S LIVING ROOM. NIGHT.

MATTHEW *is watching TV, beer in his hand, eyes glazed over.*
MARIA *comes in and sits down beside him.*

MARIA: Since when do you watch TV?

MATTHEW: It was on when I came in.

MARIA: How was work today?

MATTHEW: I don't wanna talk about it.

MARIA: I've decided to go back to high school.

MATTHEW: Why?

MARIA: I don't want to work in a factory.

MATTHEW: When we get married you won't have to work at all.

MARIA: But I want to. Just not in a factory.

MATTHEW: How can you go to high school pregnant?

MARIA: Plenty of girls do it.

MATTHEW: I can teach you everything you can learn in high school.

MARIA: I don't want that.

MATTHEW: Why?

MARIA: Because I just don't want it.

(MATTHEW *watches TV. After a while* . . .)

I met the man today.

MATTHEW: What man?

MARIA: The husband of the lady on the bench.

MATTHEW: Oh, yeah. What was he like?

MARIA: Nervous.

MATTHEW: Did you ask him if his wife stole the baby?

MARIA: You don't care, do you?

MATTHEW: Care about what?

MARIA: Can you stop watching TV for a moment?

MATTHEW: No.

MARIA: Why?

MATTHEW: I had a *bad* day. I had to subvert my principles and kowtow to an idiot. Television makes these daily sacrifices possible. It deadens the inner core of my being. (MARIA *gets up and sits right in front of the TV.*)

MARIA: Let's move away, then.

MATTHEW: They have television everywhere. There's no escape. And besides, you won't leave your mother.

MARIA: I will if you quit your job.

MATTHEW: What?

INT. MARIA'S KITCHEN. NIGHT.

JEAN *is at the sink, over-hearing* MARIA *and* MATTHEW. *She has a full bottle of gin in her hand.*

INT. MARIA'S LIVING ROOM. NIGHT.

MARIA: I don't like what's happening to you. If you don't like your job, you shouldn't do it.
(MATTHEW *registers this change in her outlook. He thinks.*)
MATTHEW: You'd leave your mother?
MARIA: I'm not doing her any good staying.
MATTHEW: After the baby?
MARIA: No. Now.
MATTHEW: Maria, having a baby costs money.

INT. MARIA'S KITCHEN. NIGHT.

JEAN *stands to the side of the entrance to the living room, eavesdropping.*
MATTHEW: (*Voice over*) In six months I'll have complete medical coverage down at the plant.

INT. MARIA'S LIVING ROOM. NIGHT.

MATTHEW: (*Continued*) I'm just trying to be practical. Levelheaded.
MARIA: What's so practical about being levelheaded?
MATTHEW: Move away from the TV. The news is on and I want to hear about the earthquake victims.
MARIA: Why? What are you going to do for them?
MATTHEW: Commiserate.
MARIA: What's "commiserate"?
MATTHEW: To express sympathy. Now move aside.
MARIA: Is that like compassion?
MATTHEW: No. Compassion means to suffer *with*. Which is different than just feeling pity. You need a thesaurus.
MARIA: A what?

MATTHEW: A thesaurus. It's like a dictionary of synonyms. (*He drains the last of his beer.*) Would you get me another beer?

MARIA: You're already drunk.

MATTHEW: No, I'm not drunk. I don't get drunk.

MARIA: Your job is making you boring and mean.

MATTHEW: My job is making me a respectable member of society.
(MARIA *gets up and puts on her jacket.*)
Where are you going?
(MARIA *doesn't answer. She just walks out of the room.*)

INT. MARIA'S KITCHEN. NIGHT – SAME TIME.

MARIA *comes in from the living room.* JEAN *is standing by the entrance sewing something.*

JEAN: Where are you going?

MARIA: To the supermarket. We need stuff.

JEAN: Come here. Your hair needs brushing.
(MARIA *hangs her head, sighs, then comes over and sits at the kitchen table.* JEAN *picks up her brush and starts . . .*)
Did you clean the bathroom?

MARIA: Yes.

JEAN: I want you to do this kitchen floor.

MARIA: I'll do it tonight when everyone's asleep.

JEAN: Did you vacuum upstairs?

MARIA: Yes.

JEAN: Change all the sheets tomorrow before you go to work and hang out the clothes that are in the washing machine.

MARIA: OK.

JEAN: When's he going to fix my sewing machine?

MARIA: You never use it.

JEAN: I don't use it because it's broken.
(MARIA *reaches back and stops the brushing.*)

MARIA: He'll get around to it. (*She heads for the door.*)

JEAN: Don't forget milk. We need milk!

INT. MARIA'S LIVING ROOM. NIGHT – A LITTLE LATER.

MATTHEW *is still watching the TV program.* JEAN *comes in and sits down next to him.*

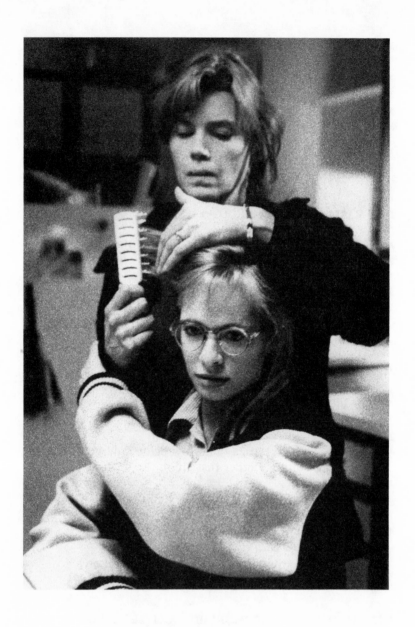

JEAN: I want you out of my house.

MATTHEW: Fine. But if I leave, Maria leaves with me.

JEAN: No chance.

MATTHEW: We can go on like this forever, Mom.

JEAN: Don't call me Mom!

MATTHEW: Like it or not: I'm here to stay.

JEAN: Freeloader.

MATTHEW: My paycheck kicks in to run this household too, you know.

JEAN: Who asked *you* for help, anyway?

MATTHEW: Maria did.

JEAN: Maria's a child.

MATTHEW: Soon to be my wife.

JEAN: (*Stunned*) Over my dead body!

MATTHEW: It's all set. We go to Town Hall on Monday.

> (JEAN *stares at* MATTHEW, *amazed*.)

You want a beer?

INT. MARIA'S KITCHEN. NIGHT – SAME TIME.

MATTHEW *opens the fridge.*

JEAN: (*Voice over*) What the hell's wrong with Peg?

MATTHEW: There's nothing wrong with Peg. I just don't want to marry her.

JEAN: (*Voice over*) Peg could take a punk like you and make a real man out of ya!

MATTHEW: I don't think I could stand being a real man, to tell you the truth.

JEAN: (*Enters*) You might be able to convince Maria to marry you, but you'll never be able to take her away from me. I know how to deal with Maria.

> (MATTHEW *looks at her. He knows she's right*.)

MATTHEW: You're a selfish bitch.

JEAN: I brought her into this world. Don't you forget that.

MATTHEW: You don't deserve her.

JEAN: Neither do you.

MATTHEW: You wanna arm wrestle about it?

> (JEAN *steps back, sizes him up a moment, then turns away*

153

and goes to the sink where she picks up a bottle of scotch and a bottle of gin.)

JEAN: We'll drink for it.

MATTHEW: What?

JEAN: We'll drink for it. Whoever's left standing, wins.

MATTHEW: Jean, I can drink you under the table.

JEAN: That's what you think. Scotch is your poison, isn't it? Mine's gin.

MATTHEW: Jean, this is going to be way too easy.

JEAN: I'll get you out of my house one way or another.

MATTHEW: You won't do it *this* way.

JEAN: You're full of hot air, pal.

MATTHEW: You'll regret this whole thing in the morning, Mom.

JEAN: Shot for shot. There are two more bottles under the sink. And don't you *ever* call me Mom.

MATTHEW: (*Lifts the bottle of scotch and takes a drink*) To motherhood.

JEAN: (*Lifts her bottle*) Bastard.

INT. DINER. NIGHT

MARIA *is sitting at the counter, reading* Man and the Universe.
*When she comes across a word she needs to look up, she writes it
down in her notebook.*
She looks up as . . .
NURSE PAINE *comes into the diner. She approaches the counter
and sits down next to* MARIA.
The COOK *behind the counter is nervous.*
PAINE: Coffee.
COOK: Look, we don't want any trouble!
PAINE: Coffee!
COOK: We're closing up.
PAINE: (*Ignores him*) Milk, no sugar.
MARIA: Hi.
PAINE: Hi.
MARIA: You work late?
PAINE: They smashed my car up again. Tipped it over into
    the street.
MARIA: Bastards.
PAINE: I'm doing what I believe in. And if you're going to *do*
    that, you've got to be ready to take a certain amount of
    shit.
MARIA: I'm going to have an abortion.
PAINE: Are you sure it's what you want?
MARIA: Yes.
PAINE: You have to be sure. You have to be sure or nothing
    ever changes. People spend their entire lives making the
    same mistakes again and again.
MARIA: I'm sure.
PAINE: Are you alone?
MARIA: I met a man.
PAINE: He knows you're pregnant.
MARIA: He wants to marry me.
PAINE: Do you want that?
MARIA: Sometimes I'm sure I do. Other times I'm not so
    certain. He's a good man. But he's out of control. It seems
    like meeting me has made him capable and ready to give
    himself. I mean, completely, you know?
PAINE: Isn't that a good thing?

155

MARIA: I like him the way he is.
PAINE: How is he?
MARIA: Dangerous. But sincere.
PAINE: Sincerely dangerous.
MARIA: No, dangerous *because* he's sincere.
PAINE: I see. And now he's becoming insincere?
MARIA: Not exactly. He's just sort of numb.
PAINE: Because you've changed him.
MARIA: I didn't mean to, honest.
PAINE: No, you didn't mean to, but still it happens. People
      change each other. People start becoming what others
      want them to be.
MARIA: I just want him to be himself.
PAINE: Impossible.
MARIA: Really?
PAINE: How can you expect him to stay the same when you've
      come into his life?
MARIA: You think I should leave him?
PAINE: Look, hasn't he changed you?
MARIA: I guess so.
PAINE: There you go.

MARIA: I don't understand.

PAINE: There's nothing to understand. (*She looks around the diner.*) Here's my husband. (*She turns and stubs out her cigarette.*)

MARIA: I'll be there tomorrow.

PAINE: (*Pauses*) As long as you know what you're doing.

MARIA: I know what I'm doing.

INT. MARIA'S KITCHEN. NIGHT.

There are two empty bottles.
Two more are half empty.
MATTHEW *and* JEAN *are sitting on the kitchen floor.*

MATTHEW: Here, let me pour you another one, Jean.

JEAN: (*Frowns*) Thanks.

    (MATTHEW *pours and hands* JEAN *the drink. She takes it, sighs, then knocks it back.* MATTHEW *screws up his face, disappointed, and pours himself another.*)

MATTHEW: (*Disturbed*) Shit.

JEAN: I've been meaning to ask you something.

MATTHEW: What's that?

JEAN: What was your mother like?

    (MATTHEW *polishes off another with some difficulty. He shakes his head clear and places the glass back on the floor.*)

MATTHEW: I don't remember her.

JEAN: You were that young when she died?

MATTHEW: She died giving birth to me.

JEAN: No.

MATTHEW: It's the truth.

JEAN: That's terrible.

MATTHEW: I agree.

JEAN: So unfair.

MATTHEW: Of course.

JEAN: I feel sorry for your father.

MATTHEW: I had a feeling you two would hit it off.

JEAN: You can't blame him for hating you.

MATTHEW: I never said he hated me.

JEAN: But you don't get along.

157

MATTHEW: No. We don't get along. But then neither do you and Maria.

JEAN: Me and Maria will get along just fine once you're out of the picture.

MATTHEW: She'll waste away here with you.

JEAN: And what the hell kinda life are you gonna be able to give her?

MATTHEW: Any kinda life she wants.

JEAN: She wants to stay with me.

MATTHEW: Says who?

JEAN: Look, let me tell you something. 'Cause, you know, it's not like I hated you right off the bat or anything.

MATTHEW: I appreciate that.

JEAN: It's just that I don't want to see Maria make the same mistake I made. And that Peg made.

MATTHEW: (*Groggy*) What mistake is that?

JEAN: Men!

MATTHEW: Oh.

JEAN: Children are OK. But marriage is always a last resort. A woman can have anything she wants. Anything. But we always make the mistake of thinking we need a man to do it.

MATTHEW: Well, I mean, correct me if I'm wrong, but . . . isn't it sort've impossible to have a baby without a man around the house?

JEAN: Wake up, Matthew, this is the twentieth century! You can be artificially inseminated! They've got sperm banks and everything! The possibilities are endless!

MATTHEW: You're out of your mind!

JEAN: I'm fed up! That's all! You know, when my husband died, sure, I was in shock. But what I really felt was relief!

MATTHEW: What!

JEAN: Relief. Yeah. That man poisoned the past twenty years of my life. Some nights I'd lay awake just hoping he'd sort've just—well disappear or something. And then WHACK! Maria, with one slap, knocks him right out of my life! Incredible! I was amazed. The girl's a genius! (MATTHEW *stares at her, stunned.*)
Do you love him?

MATTHEW: Who?

JEAN: Your father.

MATTHEW: I don't love anybody.

JEAN: Yeah, right. I keep forgetting. Drink up.

(MATTHEW *pours himself another and tries to concentrate.*)

MATTHEW: You know, with me and my dad, it was as if our relationship was a record album. You know, and the phonograph that the record was playing on had a very old and worn out needle. Know what I'm saying? There were these *skips*. Bad *skips*. These painful *gouges*. But in your *head*, you know, you compensate for it. You keep the *beat* because you know the *song*.

(JEAN *just watches him.*)

Most people buy laser discs now. CDs. They don't wear out. You can't damage the surface of CDs. They're digital. Not analog. Would you like for me to explain to you, Jean, the difference between analog and digital recording?

JEAN: No.

MATTHEW: It's really fascinating stuff.

JEAN: I'm sure it is.

MATTHEW: (*Drinks*) Jean.

JEAN: Huh.

MATTHEW: I think . . . I think I'm . . . I think I'm actually drunk.

JEAN: I think so too.

(JEAN *gives him a little nudge with her finger and . . . CRASH! Down he goes. It looks like he's passed out.* JEAN *shakes him.* MATTHEW *opens his eyes.*)

MATTHEW: What?

INT. STAIRWAY. NIGHT

JEAN *struggles up the stairs with* MATTHEW *hung over her shoulder.*

INT. PEG'S BEDROOM. NIGHT.

JEAN *slams in through the door with* MATTHEW *in tow. She heaves him across the room and tumbles him down onto . . . Peg's bed.*

159

JEAN *steps back and catches her breath, then stoops over*
MATTHEW *and listens closely to make sure he's . . .*
Sleeping. She smiles victoriously, waits a moment, then starts
undressing him. She undoes his trousers and pulls them off, takes
off his shirt, strips him completely.

INT. UPSTAIRS HALLWAY. NIGHT – MOMENTS LATER.

JEAN *closes the door. She starts up the hall, but then stops,*
remembering something. She takes the hair clip out of her hair
and goes back into the room.

INT. PEG'S BEDROOM. NIGHT – SAME TIME

JEAN *turns on the TV and places the hair clip on top of it. She*
pauses a moment and gazes at MATTHEW *lying naked under the*
sheets. She shakes her head and sighs.
MATTHEW *sleeps.*

INT. MARIA'S KITCHEN. NIGHT – MOMENTS LATER.

JEAN *enters the kitchen and stops short when she sees . . .*
PEG, *just back from work. She's holding the half-empty bottle of*
gin.
PEG: (*Gesturing toward the bottle of scotch*) What's going on
    here, Mom?
JEAN: None of your business. (*She picks up the bottle of scotch.*)
    You should've been home half an hour ago.
PEG: The other girl got sick. (*She drinks out of the gin bottle in*
    her hand.) What is this?
JEAN: What?
PEG: This isn't gin.
JEAN: Oh, that.
PEG: This is water.
JEAN: Gimme that.
PEG: Why are you watering down the gin, Mom?
JEAN: I'm not watering down the gin. I was using that to
    water the plants.

PEG: What plants?

JEAN: Will you stop asking stupid questions and just go on up to bed!

    (PEG *pours a scotch instead. Checks it, and . . .*)

PEG: Well, at least the scotch is real.

    (PEG *takes her drink and leaves the kitchen.* JEAN *stares off into space.*)

INT. STAIRWAY. NIGHT – SAME TIME.

PEG *starts up the stairs.*

INT. PEG'S BEDROOM. NIGHT – SAME TIME.

PEG *enters the room, but stops short when she sees* MATTHEW *sleeping in her bed. She quickly closes the door.*

INT. MARIA'S KITCHEN. NIGHT – SAME TIME.

JEAN *is sewing. She hears the sound of Peg's door closing.*

EXT. SUPERMARKET. NIGHT.

MARIA *comes out of the supermarket carrying her groceries.*

ANTHONY *is standing by his car.*

ANTHONY: Maria.

MARIA: What do *you* want?

ANTHONY: I wanna apologize.

MARIA: Oh, great. What happened with your football scholarship?

ANTHONY: I didn't get it. I failed my college entrance exam.

MARIA: I'm sorry to hear that.

ANTHONY: Maria, I want you to forgive me.

MARIA: (*Sighs benevolently*) Sure. Here, give me a lift.

ANTHONY: Let me take those.

MARIA: (*Giving* ANTHONY *the grocery bags*) Thanks.

ANTHONY: What did you do to your hair?

MARIA: Nothing.
ANTHONY: I didn't know you wore glasses.

INT. PEG'S BEDROOM. NIGHT – SAME TIME.

PEG *is in her slip, propped up on an elbow beside* MATTHEW. *She has her drink in her hand. She lightly slaps Matthew's face. He just moans and continues sleeping.*
PEG: Matthew. (*She waits, but there's no response. She takes out her gum and kisses* MATTHEW *on the mouth. He smacks his lips, but remains asleep.* PEG *puts her gum back in her mouth and sighs.*)

EXT. MARIA'S HOUSE. NIGHT.

ANTHONY *is trying to kiss* MARIA.
MARIA: Get your *hands* off of me, Anthony!
ANTHONY: Don't come on so high and mighty with me, Maria!
MARIA: I'm not being high and mighty. I just don't want your hands anywhere near me. Now, get me my groceries out of the trunk.
ANTHONY: It's true about you and that psycho-case, isn't it?
MARIA: What psycho-case?
ANTHONY: Matthew Slaughter.
MARIA: As a matter of fact, yes. It is. We're getting married on Monday. Now get my groceries out of the trunk.
ANTHONY: (*Stunned*) What!
MARIA: Give me the keys. I'll get them myself.
ANTHONY: You can't do that!
MARIA: Why not?
ANTHONY: What about us?
       (MARIA *looks at* ANTHONY.)

INT. MARIA'S KITCHEN. NIGHT.

MARIA *comes in the back door with the groceries, seething.*
JEAN *doesn't look up as* MARIA *drops the packages on the table.*
JEAN: It's about time. I wanted a cup of tea, but there's no milk.

(MARIA *glares sideways at* JEAN, *then slams down the quart of milk on the table.*

JEAN *starts. She watches from the corner of her eye as* MARIA *throws her jacket off and begins putting things away.*)

Maria, I left my hair clip up in Peg's room. Can you go get it for me?

(MARIA *stands for a moment and calms herself, then looks over at her mother.* JEAN *looks back at her.*)

Did you hear me?

MARIA: Why can't you get it yourself?

JEAN: (*Stunned*) What?

MARIA: Mom, you're a normal, healthy person. There's no reason for me to do every little thing for you.

JEAN: What's gotten into *you*?

MARIA: Nothing's gotten into me. I'm just telling you how it is.

(JEAN *is getting desperate.*)

JEAN: Go get my hair clip!

(MARIA *sighs and then comes over and sits at the table with* JEAN.)

MARIA: Listen, Mom. I'm sorry about Dad.

(JEAN *just stares at her.* MARIA *waits.*)

JEAN: Are you going to marry Matthew?

MARIA: Maybe.

JEAN: (*Ice cold*) It's your life. Do what you want with it.

MARIA: That's right. It's my life. And I'll do what I want with it.

(MARIA *watches her mother closely. Finally,* JEAN *looks up, pauses, and . . .*)

JEAN: Go get my hair clip.

(*They stare each other down a moment longer, then* MARIA *gets up and leaves the room.* JEAN *stares a hole in the table, deeply shaken despite her ice cold routine.*)

INT. STAIRWAY. NIGHT.

MARIA *moves up the stairs toward Peg's room.*

163

INT. MARIA'S KITCHEN. NIGHT – SAME TIME.

JEAN *doesn't blink. She waits motionlessly, her sewing frozen in
her hands. She is terribly frightened.
On the stove, the kettle starts to whistle.*
JEAN *doesn't react. She breathes in deep, waiting.
The kettle whistles . . .*

INT. STAIRWAY. NIGHT – SAME TIME.

*The empty stairway. From the kitchen we hear the kettle's shrill,
relentless whistle.*

INT. MARIA'S KITCHEN. NIGHT – SAME TIME.

JEAN *at the table, not moving; stiff as a board, waiting. The
kettle is deafening.
Jean's hands, with the sewing, slowly drop to the table.
She hangs her head there a moment, then . . .
The whistling stops.*

164

JEAN *looks up, startled.*
MARIA *is standing there, her hand still on the stove's burner knob.*
MARIA *pours a cup of tea and brings it, with the hair clip, over to the table, setting it before* JEAN.
MARIA: Here you go. I'm going to bed. Good night.
> (JEAN *sits there, uncomprehending, as* MARIA *kisses her on the head and leaves the kitchen.* MARIA *seemed completely undisturbed.* JEAN *stares at her hair clip and at the tea, puzzled.*)

INT. STAIRWAY. NIGHT – MOMENTS LATER.

JEAN *comes quietly, but determinedly, up the stairs and moves toward Peg's room.*

INT. PEG'S BEDROOM. NIGHT – SAME TIME.

JEAN *opens the door slowly.*
The hallway light falls over . . .
MATTHEW *and* PEG, *asleep together on the bed.*
JEAN *just stares at them, dumbfounded.*

INT. MARIA'S BATHROOM. NIGHT – SAME TIME.

In the shower, MARIA *is pressing her forehead into the corner of the tiled wall with her eyes shut tight and her fists clenched and held up just beneath her chin.*
The water pours down over her head.
The bathroom fills with steam.

FADE TO BLACK.

INT. CLINIC. DAY.

MARIA *is being questioned by a* NURSE. *She is wearing a hospital gown. The* NURSE *holds a clipboard.*
NURSE: Emphysema?
MARIA: No.
NURSE: Heart disease?

MARIA: No.
NURSE: Venereal disease?
MARIA: No.
NURSE: Are you allergic to penicillin?
MARIA: No.
NURSE: Other allergies?
MARIA: No.
NURSE: Have you been hospitalized for any illness within the past six months?
MARIA: No.
NURSE: Have you had an abortion before?
MARIA: No.
NURSE: Social Security number?
MARIA: Is Nurse Paine here?
NURSE: Why?
MARIA: No reason.
NURSE: She's off today. Social Security number?
MARIA: 081–50–9199.
NURSE: OK. Drink this.
MARIA: What is it?
NURSE: Just drink it and lean back.
MARIA: (*Drinks, then lies back on the table*) Will this hurt?
NURSE: Don't worry. It's a simple procedure.

INT. RUARK COMPUTER FACTORY. DAY – MEANWHILE.

The rows of WORKERS *are busy at their benches. We move along until we come to . . .*
MATTHEW *at his bench. He has an enormous hangover and has his chin propped up in his hand. His eyes are closed. He opens them gradually, rubs his forehead, takes a drag on his cigarette, and tries to start working. He lifts . . .*
The circuit board A-67-9.
He regards it for a long time.

INT. RUARK BOSS'S OFFICE. DAY – A LITTLE LATER.

The BOSS *is handing some documents to* ED *as* MATTHEW *enters. They both regard* MATTHEW *apprehensively.* ED *makes a quick exit.*

166

BOSS: Yes, Matthew?

MATTHEW: Have you got a minute?

BOSS: Sure. What is it?

MATTHEW: I just have a question. I was a little confused. The specification manual for the new model we're assembling calls for a particular piece. A circuit board. A-67-9.

BOSS: I know the piece.

MATTHEW: Well, it's just that I remember we manufactured that piece last year and an unusually high number of them checked out faulty.

BOSS: Yes, I'm aware of that.

MATTHEW: There was a defect in the pressing of the . . .

BOSS: Matthew, I *understand*.

MATTHEW: Oh.

BOSS: Matthew, listen. I appreciate your diligence. But there are people in this company, highly qualified people, people in important positions making decisions about these things. And they know what they're doing.

(MATTHEW *just stares at her, pale and ill.*)

MATTHEW: Uh huh.

BOSS: Now, if these people saw fit to include part A-67-9 in the new model, well then we have to trust that they have a reason for doing so. Agreed?

MATTHEW: (*Slowly*) Yes.

BOSS: (*Sincere*) So, Matthew, once again, thank you for your diligence and dedication, but please just go back down there and do your job.

(MATTHEW *waits a few moments before moving, staring at the floor, then* . . .)

MATTHEW: Yes, sir.

BOSS: Excuse me?

MATTHEW: I'm sorry.

BOSS: Good.

MATTHEW: I quit.

(*The* BOSS *stares at* MATTHEW *as he leaves.*)

INT. CLINIC (RECOVERY ROOM). DAY.

MARIA *sits, dressed, in an otherwise empty recovery room. She's calm and remote. A small plastic cup of orange juice is beside her. She looks up as* . . .

JEAN *comes in. She sits beside* MARIA. *They are silent for a while, then* . . .

JEAN: Do you want to go home now?

MARIA: No. I have some things to do.

(JEAN *sits there, feeling sort of useless and intensely guilty.* MARIA *senses this and takes her hand.*)

I'll be home later.

(*Finally,* JEAN *gets up and goes.* MARIA *takes something out of her pocket and looks down at* . . .

The address label from Robert's briefcase.)

EXT. ROBERT AND RACHEL'S HOUSE. DAY.

MARIA *comes up to the door and knocks. She waits. No one answers. She knocks again. Waits. She knocks a third time* . . . *The door opens a crack. She looks up and sees* . . .

ROBERT *looking out at her.*

She says nothing.

168

He says nothing. After a moment, the door slowly opens wider.
ROBERT *steps aside and* MARIA *hesitates, then enters.*
ROBERT *reaches out and takes in the mail, looking around the
neighborhood as he does so.*

INT. ROBERT AND RACHEL'S HOUSE. DAY – MOMENTS LATER.

There is a hall leading from the front door to the living room.
MARIA *moves carefully and slowly down the hall toward the living
room, as* ROBERT *brings in the newspaper and closes the door,
lingering just inside it a moment.*
MARIA *comes into the living room and finds . . .*
RACHEL *sitting alone in a chair by the window. Her hands folded
tightly before her, she stares off at nothing until, finally, she
sees . . .*
MARIA *across the room, politely keeping her distance.* ROBERT
appears behind her; nervous, helpless, a tired wreck.
RACHEL *looks away and* MARIA *approaches. She attempts to place
her hand on Rachel's shoulder, but then draws back.*
There's a thud against the table and MARIA *looks over at . . .*
The newspaper ROBERT *has tossed. Its headline reads . . .*

169

STOLEN INFANT FOUND IN PHONE BOOTH

MARIA, *amazed, looks up at* ROBERT.

ROBERT: They found him this morning. The police got an
    unidentified phone call, apparently. They say he's OK.
    Just fine.
    (ROBERT *turns and walks out of the room.*
    MARIA *watches him go, then looks back down at* . . .
    RACHEL, *who is locked in her own world.*)

INT. MARIA'S HOUSE. AFTERNOON.

MATTHEW *storms in the back door, happy. He's got a bunch of
flowers in one hand and a brand new book in the other. He slams
it down by the sink.*
It's a thesaurus.
MATTHEW *takes off his coat and throws it, with a flourish, to the
floor.*
There's someone knocking at the door.
*He goes toward the back door and when he sees who it is, with
resignation, he opens the door.*
DAD *comes in, looking up at* MATTHEW *and scratching his chin
uncertainly.*

INT. MARIA'S KITCHEN. AFTERNOON—MOMENTS LATER.

DAD *and* MATTHEW *are standing side by side against the kitchen
cabinets.*
DAD: What are you doing here?
MATTHEW: I live here.
DAD: Come on home, Matthew.
MATTHEW: No.
DAD: Matthew, I spent all my life looking out for you, now
    you desert me.
MATTHEW: The two of us are better off on our own.
DAD: You're selfish.
MATTHEW: I'm just trying to be responsible.
DAD: You're a fool, Matthew. I've heard about all this.
    Everybody knows that girl's child isn't yours.
MATTHEW: Big deal.

DAD: Big deal. She's just taking advantage of you.

MATTHEW: We better not talk about this, Dad.

DAD: You'll always be a fool, Matthew. You need someone to look after you.

MATTHEW: Why don't you just say it?

DAD: Say what?

MATTHEW: That you want me to come home because you're lonely.

DAD: Bullshit.

MATTHEW: Why don't you just say you're sorry for the way things never seem to work out between the two of us?

DAD: You're saying it's my fault?

MATTHEW: It's nobody's fault.

DAD: It's that little slut's fault! That's whose fault it is.

MATTHEW: Watch it, Dad.

DAD: Fucking low-life bitch!

MATTHEW: You better get out of here, Dad.

DAD: What are you gonna do about it?

MATTHEW: I'm warning you, Dad.

DAD: Come on. What are you gonna do about it?

MATTHEW: I swear to God, I'm going to knock you out.

DAD: Try it! I'll knock your ass through your face! Come on, try it!

(MATTHEW *sighs.*)

What's the matter? You afraid?

(*WHAM!* MATTHEW *punches* DAD *in the stomach and the older man stumbles back, amazed and a little winded.*
MATTHEW *looks on, worried.*
DAD *looks up at him, takes off his cap, and dives at his son. They go crashing down, through the kitchen table, knocking chairs over, and shaking the whole house. They roll around on the floor, punching and kicking each other with all their might.*)

EXT. MARIA'S HOUSE. DAY – SAME TIME.

JEAN *comes walking into the yard and stops when she hears the brutal sounds of fighting from inside the house: dishes smashing, furniture breaking . . .*

171

INT. MARIA'S KITCHEN. DAY — MOMENTS LATER.

MATTHEW *takes Dad's arm, opens a drawer beneath the sink, and jams Dad's hand in.*
KACHOONK! MATTHEW *slams it closed on Dad's fingers.*
They go crashing across the kitchen as JEAN *enters. She stops dead in her tracks, looking at the fight, and then runs out of the kitchen as* DAD *gets* MATTHEW *in a headlock, opens the refrigerator door, and . . .*
SLAM! He closes it against Matthew's head. DAD *staggers back and waits.*

EXT. MARIA'S HOUSE. DAY — SAME TIME.

MARIA *comes walking up to the house and stops when she sees . . .*
JEAN *standing, petrified, in the front yard. She turns and looks at* MARIA.
MARIA *hears the commotion and goes up to the house.*

172

INT. MARIA'S KITCHEN. DAY – MOMENTS LATER.

MARIA *steps carefully into the kitchen and sees . . .*
DAD *leaning over the sink, wetting a dish cloth and touching it to*
a cut on his face.
He looks over at MARIA, *slowly.*
MARIA *holds Dad's gaze a moment, then turns and walks away.*

INT. BATHROOM. DAY – MOMENTS LATER.

MARIA *comes up the stairs and finds . . .*
MATTHEW *in the bathroom, leaning over the sink, also wetting a*
towel and cleaning up cuts on his face. He looks up at her and
smiles.
MARIA *comes to him.*
MARIA: Are you OK?
MATTHEW: I quit.
MARIA: What?
MATTHEW: I quit my job.
MARIA: Why?
    (MATTHEW *sits on the edge of the tub.*)

MATTHEW: You're right. We've got to get out of here. This is no place to raise a child.

(MARIA *sits on the edge of the toilet opposite* MATTHEW.)

Maria, I woke up in Peg's bed this morning. I don't know how . . .

MARIA: Stop.

(MATTHEW *stops and looks helpless.*)

I've had an abortion.

(MATTHEW *stares at her a moment, then looks down again, crushed. She reaches out and caresses him. He hangs his head, disturbed and confused.*)

I don't want to get married.

(MARIA *holds Matthew's gaze. He looks back down and heaves a sigh. Finally, he lifts the thesaurus off the floor and hands it to her.*)

MATTHEW: I bought you this.

(MARIA *takes it, looks at it, then watches as* MATTHEW *gets up and walks out of the bathroom.*)

INT. MARIA'S KITCHEN. DAY — SAME TIME.

JEAN *stands behind* DAD, *who's sitting at the kitchen table.*

JEAN: (*Frowning*) And who do you think you are?

DAD: Leave me alone.

JEAN: Look what you've done to my cabinets.

DAD: Get me a hammer and I'll fix it.

JEAN: Do you want something to eat?

INT. MARIA'S BEDROOM. DAY.

Maria's top drawer is open. MARIA *rushes to it and looks in to see . . .*
The grenade is gone.

EXT. STREET. DAY — MOMENTS LATER.

MARIA *walks quickly up the street. A police squad car passes her with its siren blaring.*

174

EXT. RUARK COMPUTER FACTORY. DAY.

MARIA *comes rushing up to a crowd of* WORKERS *and* OTHERS, *who are all standing around at a safe distance from the factory. A few more people run out of the factory, including* ED *and the* BOSS, *who is demanding that* ED *go back into the factory and get* MATTHEW *out.*
MARIA *passes right by them and enters the factory.*

INT. RUARK COMPUTER FACTORY. DAY — MOMENTS LATER.

MARIA *rushes through the factory, finally slowing when she sees . . .*
MATTHEW *sitting on an overturned word processor, holding the grenade before him.*
MARIA *comes forward.*
MATTHEW *looks up and sees her.*
MARIA *strides bravely on and comes up to him. She stops and looks down at . . .*
The grenade in his hand, then over at . . .
The grenade's pin in his other hand.
She looks up at . . .
MATTHEW, *who looks from her to the pieces in his hand with a startled expression on his face.*
MARIA: What happened?
MATTHEW: I don't know. It must not be any good.
MARIA: Are you sure?
MATTHEW: No.
MARIA: You mean, it might still go off?
MATTHEW: I guess so.
> (MARIA *thinks. They both look up at each other.*
> MATTHEW *remains there, trapped.* MARIA *moves slowly toward him. Silence.*)

EXT. RUARK COMPUTER FACTORY. DAY — SAME TIME.

JEAN, PEG, *and* DAD *come running up and stand waiting with the* OTHERS.

175

INT. RUARK COMPUTER FACTORY. DAY – SAME TIME.

MARIA *slowly reaches over and gently lifts the grenade out of Matthew's hand.*
MATTHEW *holds his breath as he watches it rise up and . . .*
MARIA *carries it away, held out in front of her.*
MATTHEW *stands and comes in behind her as . . .*
MARIA *tosses the grenade. They turn away and shield themselves. We see the grenade fall to the floor and roll away. No explosion. They stand with their backs turned, tensed, but nothing happens and they look over their shoulders at . . .*
The grenade lying on the floor across the factory.
MARIA *and* MATTHEW *wait.*

EXT. RUARK COMPUTER FACTORY. DAY – SAME TIME.

Outside – the crowd waits.

INT. RUARK COMPUTER FACTORY. DAY – SAME TIME.

CLOSE-UP on grenade.
MARIA *and* MATTHEW *sigh with relief and take a few steps away . . .*
KABOOM! The grenade goes off and pieces of everything go flying by over their heads as they dive to the floor.

EXT. RUARK COMPUTER FACTORY. DAY – SAME TIME.

PEG *and* JEAN *faint in unison.*

INT. RUARK COMPUTER FACTORY. DAY – SAME TIME.

As the dust clears, MATTHEW *and* MARIA *are lying, head to head, on the floor.*
MATTHEW: I'm sorry. I lost my head.
MARIA: It's OK.
MATTHEW: What do we do now?
MARIA: We could run?

MATTHEW: We'd never make it.

MARIA: I'll tell them it was my fault.

MATTHEW: They'll never believe you.

MARIA: I don't care if they believe me or not.

MATTHEW: Why have you done this?

MARIA: Done what?

MATTHEW: Why do you put up with me like this?

MARIA: Somebody had to.

MATTHEW: But why you?

MARIA: I just happened to be here.

> (MATTHEW *is pulled to his feet by two* POLICEMEN.
> MATTHEW *stares at* MARIA *as he is being dragged away.*
> MARIA *returns his look.*)

EXT. RUARK COMPUTER COMPANY. DAY — A LITTLE LATER.

MATTHEW, *handcuffed, is led to a squad car. The door is opened for him and they start to thrust him in, but he looks back at . . .*

MARIA *as she steps forward, away from* JEAN, PEG, DAD, *and the* OTHERS.

MATTHEW *holds her gaze a moment until, finally, they manage to shove him into the back seat of the squad car. But he twists himself around and looks out the back window at . . .*

MARIA *gazing bravely back at him.*

They slam the squad car door and peel out as they start away.

MARIA *walks slowly forward after the car as it . . .*

Speeds away down the road. MATTHEW *is still peering out at her through the back window and . . .*

MARIA *steps out into the street and walks on after the car, straining to see him as . . .*

He moves farther and farther off down the road.

MARIA *walks on a little farther, straining her eyes, finally stopping to put on . . .*

CLOSE-UP: *Her glasses.*

The squad car moves even farther off into the distance, but . . .

EXTREME CLOSE-UP: MARIA *remains focused on . . .*

The spot where the car and MATTHEW *finally disappear over the horizon.*

HOLD *on* MARIA *in the middle of the road, looking off after him.*

178

Hal Hartley Filmography

As screenwriter/director unless stated:

1984
Kid
Producer: Hal Hartley
Cinematographer (16 mm color): Michael Spiller
Editor: Hal Hartley
Assistant camera and makeup/costume: Carla Gerona
Cast: Ricky Ludwig (*Ned*), Leo Gosse (*Ned's father*), Janine Erickson
    (*accordion girl*), Karen Sillas (*Patsy*), Bob Gosse (*Bruce*), George
    Feaster (*Ivan*), Pamela Stewart (*Ivan's sister*), David Troup (*the
    boyfriend*)
33 mins

1987
The Cartographer's Girlfriend
Producer: Hal Hartley
Cinematographer (16 mm color): Michael Spiller
Production designer: Carla Gerona
Editor: Hal Hartley
Cast: Marissa Chibas (*girl*), Steven Geiger (*boy*), George Feaster
    (*George*), Lorraine Achee (*Mom*), Robert Richmond (*Dad*),
    Karen Sillas, David Troup, Rick Groel
29 mins

1988
Dogs
Producer: Hal Hartley
Screenwriters: Hal Hartley, Steven O'Connor, Richard Ludwig
Cinematographer (super-8 color): Steven O'Connor
Art director: Liz Hazan
Cast: Ricky Ludwig, Mike Brady, Gary Sauer
20 mins

1989
The Unbelievable Truth
Production company: Action Features
Producers: Bruce Weiss, Hal Hartley
Executive producer: Jerome Brownstein

Cinematographer (color): Michael Spiller
Production designer: Carla Gerona
Editor: Hal Hartley
Music: Jim Coleman, Phillip Reed (guitarist), Wild Blue Yonder, the
    Brothers Kendall
Cast: Adrienne Shelly (*Audry Hugo*), Robert Burke (*Josh Hutton*),
    Christopher Cooke (*Vic Hugo*), Julia McNeal (*Pearl*), Mark
    Bailey (*Mike*), Gary Sauer (*Emmet*), Katherine Mayfield (*Liz
    Hugo*), David Healy (*Todd Whitbread*), Matt Malloy (*Otis*), Edie
    Falco (*Jane, the waitress*), Jeff Howard (*irate driver*), Kelly
    Reichardt (*his wife*), Ross Turner (*their son*), Paul Schultze
    (*Bill*), Mike Brady (*Bob*), Bill Sage (*Gus*), Tom Thon (*news
    vendor*), Mary Sue Flynn (*girl at counter*)
90 mins

1990
Trust
Production company: Zenith Productions Ltd./True Fiction Pictures
    in association with Film Four International
Producer: Bruce Weiss
Executive Producer: Jerome Brownstein
Line Producer: Ted Hope
Cinematographer (color): Michael Spiller
Production designer: Daniel Ouellette
Editor: Nick Gomez
Music: Phillip Reed, the Great Outdoors
Cast: Adrienne Shelly (*Maria Coughlin*), Martin Donovan (*Matthew
    Slaughter*), Rebecca Nelson (*Jean Coughlin*), John MacKay (*Jim
    Slaughter*), Edie Falco (*Peg Coughlin*), Gary Sauer (*Anthony*),
    Matt Malloy (*Ed*), Susanne Costollos (*Rachel*), Jeff Howard
    (*Robert*), Karen Sillas (*Nurse Paine*), Tom Thon (*deli man*),
    M. C. Bailey (*Bruce*), Patricia Sullivan (*Ruark boss*), Marko
    Hunt (*John Coughlin*), John St. James (*Mr. Santiago*), Kathryn
    Mederos (*factory woman*), Bill Sage (*John Bill*), Julie Sukman
    (*biker mom*), Robby Anderson (*Joey Blech*), Christopher Cooke
    (*diner guy*), Bea Delizio (*woman on couch*), Tamu Favorite
    (*salesgirl*), Leo Gosse (*Uncle Leo*), Elizabeth Gouse (*Grace Blech*),
    Mildred Jones (*nurse no. 2*), Pathena Parish (*factory girl*), Scott
    Robinson (*bartender*), Nena Segal (*Aunt Fay*), Jean Kay Sifford
    (*Lori*), Pamela Stewart (*Mrs. Blech*)

1991
Theory of Achievement
Production company: Yo Productions Ltd. #2/Alive from Off Center
Producers: Ted Hope, Larry Meistrich
Cinematography (color): Michael Spiller
Production designer: Steven Rosenzweig
Editor: Hal Hartley
Music: Jeffrey Howard, Ned Rifle, John Stearns
Cast: Bob Gosse, Jessica Sager, Jeffrey Howard, Elina Lowensohn,
      Bill Sage, Naledi Tshazibane, M. C. Bailey, Nick Gomez,
      Ingrid Rudfors
17.45 mins

Ambition
Production company: Good Machine, Inc., and Twin Cities Public
      Television, Inc./Alive from Off Center
Producers: Ted Hope, James Schamus
Executive producer: Alyce Dissette
Associate producer: Larry Meistrich
Cinematography (color): Michael Spiller
Production designer: Steven Rosenzweig
Editor: Hal Hartley
Music: Ned Rifle
Cast: George Feaster, Patricia Sullivan, Rick Groel, Jim McCauley,
      David Troup, Chris Buck, Margaret Mendelson, Julie Sukman,
      Lasker, Bill Sage, Larry Meistrich, Michael McGarry, Casey
      Finch, Adam Bresnick, Elizabeth Feaster, Francie Swift, Lisa
      Gorlitsky, Mark V. Lake, Bob Gosse, Ernesto Gerona, Nancy
      Kricorian
9 mins

Surviving Desire
Production company: True Fiction Pictures Ltd./American Playhouse
Producer: Ted Hope
Executive producer: Jerome Brownstein
Cinematography (color): Michael Spiller
Production designer: Steve Rosenzweig
Editor: Hal Hartley
Music: Ned Rifle, the Great Outdoors
Cast: Martin Donovan (*Jude*), Mary Ward (*Sofie*), Matt Malloy
      (*Henry*), Rebecca Nelson (*Katie*), Julie Sukman (*Jill*), Thomas J.
      Edwards, George Feaster, Lisa Gorlitsky, Emily Kunstler, John
      MacKay, Jim McCauley, Vinny Rutherford, Gary Sauer, Steve

183

Schub, Patricia Sullivan, David Troup, the Great Outdoors
(Hub Moore, John Sharples, Dan Castelli, Craig Adams)
60 mins

1992
Simple Men
Production company: Zenith Productions Ltd./American Playhouse
   Theatrical Films in association with Fine Line Features, Film
   Four International, BIM Distribuzione
Producers: Ted Hope, Hal Hartley
Executive producers: Jerome Brownstein, Bruce Weiss
Cinematography (color): Michael Spiller
Production designer: Dan Ouellette
Editor: Steve Hamilton
Music: Ned Rifle
Cast: Robert Burke (*Bill McCabe*), Bill Sage (*Dennis McCabe*), Karen
   Sillas (*Kate*), Elina Lowensohn (*Elina*), Martin Donovan
   (*Martin*), M. C. Bailey (*Mike*), Christopher Cooke (*Vic*), Jeffrey
   Howard (*Ned Rifle*), Holly Marie Combs (*Kim*), Joe Stevens
   (*Jack*), Damian Young (*Sheriff*), Marietta Marich (*Mom*), John
   MacKay (*Dad*), Bethany Wright (*Mary*), Richard Reyes (*security
   guard*), James Hansen Prince (*Frank*), Ed Geldart (*cop at desk*),
   Vivian Lanko (*nun*), Alissa Alban (*waitress*), Margaret A.
   Bowman (*Nurse Louise*), Jo Perkins (*Nurse Otto*), Mary
   McKenzie (*Vera*), Matt Malloy (*boyish cop*)
104 minutes